D0851522

For Randye ~

a grief sublime

Ben R~
12/7/19

for steve.

and for gabrielle, ari, and noah.

First Edition

Copyright © 2019 Beth Robbins

Printed in the United States

ISBN: 978-1-7340899-0-5 (Paperback)
ISBN: 978-1-7340899-1-2 (e-Book)

Library of Congress Control Number: 2019915123

Editing: Laura Didyk, Cathy Fracasse,
Meryl Joseph, Nina Ryan
Art Direction: Gabrielle Senza
Layout and Design: Devon Farber
Illustration: Gabrielle Meyerowitz

KEATS & COMPANY
PUBLISHERS

Keats & Company Publishers, LLC
PO Box 1100, Great Barrington, MA 01230
info@keatsandcompanypublishers.com
1.877.294.7747

keatsandcompanypublishers.com

TABLE OF CONTENTS

[*preamble*]

Translation derives from Middle English,

meaning to carry over.

I translate my life with Steve, and my life without

Steve. I carry it over.

I carry it across.

[before]

Shadow time. A borderlands moment. A pause.
Dusk. Early September. A muggy night. It is still
light out, a silvery hued light. Off somehow, but
a storm has been predicted, and it certainly feels
like one is coming. I curl up on the couch with
a glass of white wine, and set it on the coffee
table. I light a candle. Steve will be home soon,
but for now I am alone. It is so warm. The ceiling
fan circles slowly. Silently. The golden orb of the
porch light shimmers through the screen door.
The air is heavy. Things seem muffled.

The candle flickers. But there is no wind.
Everything feels hushed.

1

fracture

[-medusa]

Police lights. In my driveway.
Flashing. Red lights.

I am in my pajamas. It is ten at night. The glass
of white wine on the coffee table is untouched.
Steve is hours late. The lights flash red.

I think: don't answer the door.

I hear a car door slam. Then another.

Two men are on my porch. They are under the
light from the porch. They are outside my screen
door. Under the golden light from the porch.
The red lights flash from their car.
And they see me.

I turn to stone.

[a first liminal moment]

This is not my story.

This cannot be my story.

This is my story:

It was just this morning. Steve ran out. Smiling.

Noah and I were late to school. I waved.

Impatient. No time to pause for a hug, or

another wave.

I'll see you tonight after my meeting,

he called out.

Midway on our life's journey I found myself in dark woods, the right road lost.

This is my story:

I stood in front of my students. I quoted Dante.

We don't know what's going on here. . . We don't know. Our life is a faint tracing on the surface of mystery.

I quoted Annie Dillard.

I spoke about attentiveness. I spoke about the world sparking and flaming. I spoke about being lost but with attention finding a way out. Of the truth that we live in a created world.

This is my story.

Or, rather, this was my story.

But then it wasn't my story.

Steve didn't arrive home.

And a police car in the driveway.

And then the knock on the door.

If I don't open the door this will not be my story.

My story will pick up as it had been.

Like this:

He will come home. I will drink the wine. He will eat coffee ice cream.

But they knock again.

[medusa, continued]

The officers stand outside my screen door.
Under the light from the porch. They see me.

There is a feeling of unreality. A haunting. I feel
I've stepped outside of life and am entering
another realm.

I ignore the men outside.

But they do not leave.

I watch myself outside of myself.

I see myself pull my robe closed. The
movements agonizingly slow. I see myself
move from the couch toward the men.

I open the door.

The older of the two officers speaks. The
younger seems frightened. He never speaks.

Do you know Steve Meyerowitz?

Yes. He's my husband.

He was in a car accident.

[*stanza*]

Stanza is the recurring metrical unit in a poem.

It allows the reader to move with the poet,

traveling through the landscape of the poem

created. I have always thought of the word

stanza as a noun; in other words, an object.

A something. A measurable moment in

time, contained.

But it can also act as an adjective–*stanzaed*,

or *stanzaic*. It can describe something.

Stanzaic Beth hears something

incomprehensible.

The word stanza is Italian in origin, dating to the

late 16th century, and it means standing place.

Or, a pause.

2
the messengers

Shakespeare,
King Lear

Howl, howl, howl, howl! Oh, you men are made
of stone! If I were you with eyes and a tongue to
speak with, I'd crack heaven wide open with my
laments! She's gone forever. I know how to tell
when someone is alive or dead. She's as dead
as the cold ground. Let me borrow a mirror. If
her breath steams up the glass, then she's alive.

[a liminal moment, continued]

Dead?

No.

This would not be my story.

This cannot be my story.

This is not my story.

My story is this:

Steve comes home. Smiling.

Hi, Buddy!

That is my story.

Steve's hand on my head.

Hi, Buddy.

Packages dropped on the kitchen counter.

Cabinets opened. Slammed closed.

Hi, Buddy.

[the meeting]

1982. Barnard College. Senior year. I hear a lecture on Gandhi and nonviolence, and decide to become a vegetarian. After class, my friend and I go to the diner where we'd been enjoying lunches, generally burgers and fries, for the last few years. That day, the newly anointed vegetarian does not know what to eat. Even the fries are cooked in oil with beef. I eat a bun and some iceberg lettuce.

I struggle for weeks with this decision. My diet is primarily bread and chips. I am hungry.

During lunch one day I mention that I need a job and Alicia suggests I meet a friend of hers who is looking for an assistant in his home office. Her friend is known as the Sproutman and holds classes in his Riverside Drive apartment. She knows I am lost in terms of knowing what to eat and thought Sproutman might be able to help with that, too.

Sproutman and I set a time to meet, and I go to his apartment.

I remember the elevator—built in the years before World War II. Gray and small, able to accommodate no more than two adults. I remember the hallway. Gray, too. Dim lights.

When he answers the door, I step outside of my life as I had been living it.

A tortured intellectual, pseudo-goth, black-clothed, Doc Martens-wearing Barnard woman, I survived on coffee, beer, and the darkness and heaviness I found in Russian literature.

I see a man wearing a gauzy pink shirt. Sandals.
Yoga pants. A crystal around his neck. He is clear
bright joyful. Shimmering, really.

And I am none of those things.

That I might
drink, and leave
the world
unseen,
And with thee
fade away into
the forest dim.

Meeting Steve, welcomed into his apartment
filled with sun and sprouts and plants, and
crystals, framed photos of Laurel and Hardy,
Maurice Chevalier, and Pinocchio, I cross the
threshold that will come to mark my salvation.

[grief : a rehearsal]

It was only that morning.

I see you.

Sitting on the chair, the one you said was

uncomfortable.

On the mantle above you to your right sits the

metal tin that holds our dog Jack's ashes.

He had died a few weeks earlier. We hadn't

decided what to do with the ashes.

You had put a small stuffed dog on top of the tin.

[jack]

Three weeks before you died, I was teaching and you called the school.

I was called to the phone.

You were sobbing. I could not understand you.

Jack died. He died. He died in the car. On the way to the vet.

You sobbed.

Where are you, I asked.

I pulled over, you said. What do I do?

Oh, Steve. Darling. Drive the dog to the vet. They'll know what to do.

But he died, you sobbed. I carried him into the car. He was too ill to even walk. But he tried. He was such a good dog. He couldn't even stand. But he tried.

I failed him, you said.

[*proposal*]

You propose to me in Charleston, South Carolina. Near a fountain in a park. I don't know if the proposal has caught you as a surprise. You seem somewhat unprepared.

The sun is bright and everything feels happy. You look at me and ask, in an offhand sort of way, what if we got married?

Yes. I say, yes. Of course, yes.

I have no ring, you say.

Oh, that's fine, I say. I don't need a ring.

[*wedding, the first*]

March 8, 1986. It was outside near a pond in the
Berkshires with a Justice of the Peace and two
witnesses who we had never seen before and
would never see again. Until our boys, Ari and
Noah, discovered the wedding certificates (both
of them), after the accident, this first wedding
was a secret. It was before the June wedding
three months later at The Terrace Restaurant
in Manhattan.

We chose June 1 based entirely on venue
availability and convenience. Then Steve
checked the date with his astrologer. It was
not the most propitious date, Joe told him.

It would present challenges on every level--
relational, financial, and more.

Steve was immovable. He refused to marry unless the stars aligned. I was also adamant. How could we change the date? Everything was set. And no one would be receptive to our reason for switching. Including me.

Steve followed up with Joe. What if we married on the better date, the date that Joe had recommended, March 8, and then married again in June?

That would solve the problem, Joe said. The first wedding would be the one that solidified our commitment.

We decided not to share this with anyone. I felt my parents might feel betrayed, like they'd missed the real ceremony for our union.

Steve and I married, March 8, outside, near a pond in Sheffield. I was giddy. I laughed throughout our vows.

[the messengers]

Two uniformed men stand under the light,
at the threshold.

One an older gentleman, soon to retire. The
other, a young man, just getting started. A
young man who would die in a car accident one
year later. A young man who never crossed the
threshold, never walked into my home.

I begin to pace. I no longer fit in my body.

Ma'am, the older gentleman says. Ma'am? Is
there someone we can call to come and
be with you?

I see myself. I look around the hallway. I look at
our couch. I need to sit. But I don't know how.
Who can I call? I can't remember anyone's

phone number.

Ma'am?

I call my older son Ari. No answer.

I call my brother. No answer.

I call Alison. I call Janet. I call Susan. I call Cathy.
I call Christine. No answer.

No one answers their phones anymore, I say lightly.

I won't leave you until you are okay, the older man
says. I fall into him. His arms are there.

I sit down on the bottom step of our stairway.

The only person I want to call is the one person
I cannot.

[alone]

*There was a
darkness, call it
solitude,
Or blank
desertion, no
familiar shapes
Of hourly objects,
images of trees,
Of sea or sky, no
colours of green
fields;
But huge and
mighty Forms that
do not live
Like living men
mov'd slowly
through the mind
By day and were
the trouble of
my dreams.
(Wordsworth)*

Age 9. It would happen while crossing a
neighbor's yard. In the fall when darkness came
early. It wasn't dark, but was becoming dark--
that potent dusk moment. I'd be walking alone
through the yard, after Hebrew school, and
feel panic. Alone. Surrounded by the trees in
my neighbor's yard, I felt thrown instead into a
dense dangerous forest. I wanted to run, but was
too frightened to run.

Sepia-toned. A haunted place. Perilous. A
faery land, forlorn. Trees creating a canopy and
blocking the light. Vines and branches trip me.
A dog barks.

Blank incomprehensible desertion.

[gathering , part the first]

The children.

I needed the children.

Our children.

I left a message for Ari. He was at his

girlfriend's house.

Call me back, I said. It's important.

Come home, I said. It's important.

He called. He would come home.

I could not reach Noah. He was at a camp high

in the mountains. Orientation for the new school

year. No cell service. And no one answering the

phone in the camp office.

I called my friend Liz. Her husband

Curtis answered.

I can't understand you, he said.

What are you saying?

I told him again. And again.

Liz just took a sleeping pill. I'll come.

Curtis arrived.

Ed arrived.

They tried to reach Noah.

My brother arrived.

Ari arrived.

Ari, I said. Daddy was in a car accident. He died.

Ari moaned.

Ari collapsed.

Sobbing.

I still could not reach Noah.

I called Gabrielle.

Gabrielle, I said.

I have terrible news, I said.

Your father.

Yes? She said.

He died in a car accident, I said.

No. She cried.

No.

Gabrielle sobbed.

I put her on the phone with Ari.

I still could not reach Noah.

I called Steve's brother, Rick.

Rick, I said.

Rick.

Steve was in a terrible car accident.

He died.

Can you come here?

Please?

Now, please.

Yes, he said.

Yes.

I don't phone my mother. Not now.
I would wait until the morning.
I phoned my father. Or, someone did.
I don't recall.

It becomes muddled here.

Maybe Ed reached the teacher at the orientation.
He would drive Noah home.

The rabbis arrived.

Were the police here? When did they leave? The
one whose arms were there when I fell toward
him. The younger one who wouldn't come in.

Keith drove Noah down the mountain in the
school bus.

Noah's here, someone said.

I walked out onto the porch. The light seemed too bright. The air still felt thick. I could hardly breathe. Ari stood with me. We saw Noah. He jumped off the bus and ran toward the house.

Tell me, he said. Where is daddy? Tell me.

Oh, Noah. Noah.

Tell me. Just tell me.

Daddy is dead.

[gathering, part the second]

In the morning, he was alive.

In the afternoon, he was alive.

In the evening, he was dead.

It was and is and continues to be an

unfathomable incomprehensible baffling truth.

Rick called his brother Joel.

Joel howled. Their baby brother died.

Rick called me back that night.

I'll come up first thing tomorrow, he said.

With Gabrielle.

Joel will come, too.

My father in Florida said, I will fly to

you tomorrow.

All night people came and went.

The next morning I phoned my mother.

I need to tell you something. Please come over.

Tell me now, she said.

I can't. You need to come over.

Why, she asked. She was angry. Why do I need
to come now?

She was angry.

Just come, I pleaded.

She arrived. Frantic. Still angry.

What? What is it?

Steve. I said. Steve is dead.

No.

She howled.

She collapsed into my arms.

Not Steve. Not Steve. Oh, no. Not Steve. Not
Steve.

Not Steve.

[us: in the city]

We move in together in 1984. I give up my
apartment and we settle into yours. Your
Sprout House classes are very popular. It isn't
unusual to have upwards of twenty people
show up in our apartment to take your classes
in indoor gardening, cooking, fasting, juicing,
and more. You are a leader, a celebrity, a health
guru. Sprouts grow in containers on surfaces
everywhere. The refrigerator has raw foods–
carrots, Rejuvelac, bags of sprouts. You have
assistants who arrive early and help set the
space and prepare the food. I have come to
love the food you make–cashew cheese, sprout
pizza, banana ice cream. And the salads. Huge,
abundant, bursting with life. I am no
longer hungry.

But I also keep food and drink in our refrigerator

and cabinets that I still love. Coffee. Cheese.
Bread. Beer.

On the days you have morning classes, I prepare
my coffee in our bedroom with the door closed.
I set the coffee pot on the ledge, open the
window, and brew my coffee while you pour
Rejuvelac and tea for your students in the
living room.

[gathering, part the third]

It continued.

People arriving, I mean.

Rick arrived.

Gabrielle was with him. So were his two children.

And Gabrielle's partner.

I ran out to greet them.

And next to me I saw Steve. A big smile. Wearing

his bright hat.

Ari saw him in the kitchen.

Noah saw him there, too.

The immediate days after the accident.

Movement all around me. A river of people,

almost. Not overflowing the banks. But pretty

close to flooding.

My house was no longer my house. People arriving. The dishes washed, put away. A friend arriving with a bucket and soap. Mopping the floor. Flowers in vases in the kitchen. On the counter. On the table.

Apples. Oranges. Onions. Boxes of tissues. Peach pie. Apple pie. Toilet paper. Seltzer. Wine.

A child I barely knew cleaned out my refrigerator.

I thought, Steve would love all these people here. A party.

Sitting on the couch and talking about Steve. Did you know he was a performer? Did you know he was able to walk on his hands?

The friend who arrived and wailed.

The friend who told me Steve spoke to her
after he died.

And then, this: the shocking emptiness of the
house. No one. And listening to Astaire. Dancing
by myself. Tears. Sobs. Panic.

Casseroles.

Lasagna.

My life became something I floated on top of.
Or was carried through, by friends.

I write about Steve's death and post it online.
I wanted people to know Steve.

And the rituals I had paid so little attention to in
Judaism. Those rituals created a scaffolding.

[—the body]

These are the things you need to do when your spouse dies in a car accident.

- Call the police in the neighboring state where the accident occurred to find out where your husband's body is.
- Learn to refer to your husband as a body.
- Get power of attorney.
- Learn what power of attorney means.
- Get the death certificate. In fact, get many copies of the death certificate. Because anything that was in your husband's name needs to be changed to yours, and to do that you need a death certificate.
- Learn to sleep alone in the bed you shared.
- Go to Social Security to arrange for benefits your 16-year-old son is entitled to.
- Go to the Social Security office and realize you

are sobbing. In front of the representative. Who has a box of tissues on hand.

- Notice all the things that he took care of that you had no idea he was taking care of. This includes, but is not limited to: the plumbing; dealing with the septic tank when it backs up and floods the kitchen; arranging for the lawn to be mowed; paying bills, such as utilities and the mortgage; also food shopping, which was Steve's job.

- Get used to the idea that the first thing people think when they see you is, oh, that's the widow of the man who died in the car accident. Expect for this to last one year. If you live in a small town, it will last even longer.

- When the hospital calls and asks where you want "the body" taken, decide which funeral home you want. This decision is probably made without knowing anything about any of the funeral homes.

- Choose a casket. (Metal? Oak? Mahogany? Walnut? Pine? Lined? Unlined?) Learn that they are significantly more expensive than you would ever imagine.
- Decide whether your husband would want to be cremated or buried.
- Fill out the paperwork with the funeral home. This includes finding out your spouse's parents' names and birth dates. You do this by phoning your husband's older brother.
- Visit the cemetery with your children to look at options for a burial spot, and choose one.
- Decide how many plots to purchase at the cemetery. Consider planning ahead for once.
- If you choose to purchase two plots and the second one is for you, the sole surviving parent, are you going to have a headstone that lists both you and your husband's names? But you'll have your death date blank, of course.

- Look at your children when you make this decision. Look at their faces.
- Speaking of headstones, do you want one that stands up or one that is in the ground?
- What font do you want your husband's name written in? What size?
- What do you do with your husband's vitamins?
- What do you do with your husband's shoes?
- If your husband ran his own business, find people who can help you deal with that. All of it. There is so much paperwork.
- Realize that as the sole proprietor no one is authorized to sign anything related to the business except for your dead spouse.
- Become fast friends with your estate lawyer.
- Learn what an estate lawyer does.
- Notice that your car has no gas.
- It snows and your car is covered in snow. And you are late for school. And your husband is

not around to help dig out.

- Realize you don't like this new reality.
- Realize you are having trouble breathing.
- Take your friend's advice and go to a therapist. Discover that the therapist causes you more pain, saying repeatedly, you've been robbed. *You've been robbed.*
- Start to notice everything that might be seen as a sign that your husband is nearby. This includes, but is not limited to: a monarch butterfly; a red-tailed hawk; a turkey vulture; a sudden wind storm.

[*danielle*]

The arrival of a friend. Or friends.

At the exact moment you need them.

Danielle sent a text the day after the accident.
Did I want her to come and stay with me?

Yes.
Come.
Please come.

And Danielle came.

I was cushioned—yes—but I was drowning.
Flailing. Nothing to hold onto. Danielle held me.
Danielle was there. Just that. She was there. She
slept in my bed. She knew when to put a hand
on my back. To help me find my way. To me. To

my now. And from that place, to be able to listen and be present for our children.

Old English *frēond*, of Germanic origin; related to Dutch *vriend* and German *Freund*, from an Indo-European root meaning to love.

[the shirt]

When you died, Ed asked me to choose an
outfit for you. For when we would visit you in
the funeral home.

Your closet was filled with bright colors, loudly
patterned shirts. Mostly yellow.

One day, years back, you brought home a
Hawaiian shirt. Its yellows and purples were
mostly absorbed onto a black background, the
brightness muted. You were thrilled to show it
to me, thinking it a compromise.

You loved wearing it, but held back because you
knew I hated it.

Here, I said, handing it to Ed. He loved this shirt.

After you died I painted the inside of the house.

I chose the richest, most saturated colors--blue

and green and yellow and red. And orange in

the entryway. I chose the loudest and brightest

colors. I chose without hesitation. Colors that

spoke to each other.

And the house buzzed. Shimmered. It sparked.

Brilliant orange welcomed us home.

A rich blue cushioned us in the parlor. Most

nights you sat in there with Noah. The two of you

on the couch, side by side. Working. Watching

clips from the Marx Brothers, or the Three

Stooges. The room you both laughed in.

Sparkles of light.

Sparks.

Without you physically present, I hungered for color.

When we walked into the room at the funeral home, I felt such eagerness. I would see you. I had been missing you so much. You were wearing your shirt. You seemed to have some sort of padding on your body. That's the dry ice, I was told.

A red light softened everything. I know this because Rick pointed it out.

You can touch him, the funeral home director said. Here. She folded back the blanket and pulled out your right arm, resting it gently on the blanket.

He looks well, she said.

You were cold. But soft. So soft.

I held your hand. I began to rub your arm.

Ari sat down in a chair. Unable to stand.

Noah stood by my side. Silent.

Your brown eyes were closed.
Your lips were closed. Sewn shut.
No sparkle. No spark.

I held your right hand. The left was under the
blanket. Those fingers. Graceful. Tender. Magic
hands. Hands that knew how to dance over
the keys of our piano. "42nd Street." "Cheek to
Cheek." "My Buddy." Hands that held my head
when I was in labor with Ari. Hands that stroked
my face. Don't worry, Bud. It's all right. You'll
be all right.

Hands that could fix a motor. Draw pictures that made the children happy.

Hands that tended sprouts. Rinsing them. Harvesting.

Hands that sewed buttons. Hems.

Hands that held Gabrielle. Ari. Noah.

Hands that cut the cord when Noah was born.

Hands that held me.

And then, Ari spoke. I just got an email, he said. The obituary.

Should I read it here? I asked.
Here. Now. You were so cold. A cold I had never felt before.

A not living cold.

Why not, your brother said.

And so I did.

[*flight*]

There's a picture of Steve that was taken, I
believe, by Gabrielle. He looks to be about 45,
maybe younger. Steve was pretty ageless. He's
standing at the top of a mountain, perched on
the edge of a boulder. He is standing on one
foot. Perfectly balanced. And right on the edge.
His arms are spread wide. A glorious smile. He's
wearing one of his colorful hats. He looks like
he's about to soar.

No, he is soaring. Yes. He most definitely
is soaring.

He is between realms. And safe. Grounded.
Yet soaring.

[*shirt, part two*]

June 2017. Steve had been dead for just under two years. Noah graduated high school and I invited friends to our house to celebrate. Ed said he had a gift for Noah.

What is it?

The shirt.

Ed had kept Steve's clothing for us in a paper bag. Steve had been ritually prepared for burial, in a simple white shroud. With his hat. And with Jack's ashes. We had finally realized what we needed to do with them.

I repeatedly told Ed that I did not want the shirt. But also I did not want the shirt thrown away.

Does Noah want it?

I asked.

Yes. Noah wanted it.

And so at Noah's high school graduation, in
addition to gifts of books and gift certificates,
Noah received the gift of the shirt his father wore
before the burial.

The shirt is in the paper bag Ed brought over.
And it sits in Noah's room. On a shelf.

3

an interlude

[bereaved]

Bereaved speaks to a profound absence.
It is experienced especially due to a loved
one's death.

The origin of the word translates as to deprive.

Who deprives one of that beloved?

Some days are harder than others.

[cave, part the first]

I exist. I sit in my cave. I like it in my cave. I leave because I must. But I yearn for the isolation and protection of my cave. The darkness. The warmth and protection.

Alone in my cave I am at peace. The golden walls soothe and calm. The fire warms. I cuddle under my blanket. I wear woolens on my feet. A lovely soft cardigan. I can breathe.

But I am called to leave. To be in the world.
To work.

When I leave I am naked. Exposed. Raw.

And when I leave? Tears. They come. A lot.

[*inanna*]

From the great heaven, the queen of heaven,

the goddess Inanna, set her mind on the

great below.

She abandoned heaven.

She abandoned earth

She descended to the underworld.

Listen, Inanna is instructed. Listen and you can

hear. The Sumerian word for listen is wisdom. So,

yes, listening.

And silence in which to hear.

Transmutation is related to the alchemical

process of changing base metals into gold. Or,

a physical being into a spirit being. Both must

have the potential for the apparent higher form

within. Metals somehow containing gold.

Inanna moves into a realm which is not earth and not heaven. It is the underworld. I'd never understood that before. The underworld is, it seems, a liminal space. Not this nor that. But other. And both. Movement between. In and out.

No sight
No hearing
No touch
No speech

A realm or a moment of negatives.

Orpheus descends. He must save Eurydice.
He loves Eurydice. He longs for Eurydice.
He is granted his wish. But don't look back,
he is cautioned.

Of course he looks back.

Such a human action. To walk knowing the
beloved is there behind, but not being able
to be seen, or for you to see the longed for,
mourned for, other. Of course he looks back.

Lot's wife is told. You will be saved. But don't
look back.

Of course she looks back.

Her home is being destroyed. The people she
left behind were in that city that she was not to
look toward.

Only to move forward? Is it not possible to
look back?

I drown. I become a pillar of salt. I lose the man
who walks behind me. Because I don't have the
deep knowing that he is with me. Right with me.

Present. Yet unseen.

Inanna has to lose everything that is external
to her. With every step she has a part of herself
taken. Her crown. Her cloak. The outer garments
that identify her as queen. But then it is her
physical body. One part at a time. Her arm. Her
other arm. Her leg. Her other leg. When she
makes it to the depths of the underworld she
is just a slab. She is hung onto a meat hook.
No longer the queen, Innana is a limbless,
headless slab.

And how is she saved? By another who
remembers her. That is how she is re/membered.

Who am I? Who is Steve, even now?

What was our relationship? What is our
relationship?

It must all be re/membered. All of it.

And it is a difficult scary painful journey. All the outer garments are stripped away.

And when there is nothing left, what is there? No thing. But still the self remains. Emptied, stripped of the temporal. It is the moment when I step off the cliff into this world I no longer know. I am thrust back to myself. But where am I hiding?

[a lover's discourse]

Discourse is conversation, dialogue. It derives from late Middle English denoting the power of reasoning.

The origin of the word derives from the verb *discurrere*, to run away.

Losing assumed identities, stripping away the layers that disguise the self--this is what grief has given.

This journey through grief has thrown me back on Beth. I am surrounded by people, but alone and isolated in grief. So much of the time it feels as if here now there is no comfort.

Because the one that could comfort left.

I find myself in a landscape unexplored,

unknown. And I need to navigate on my own.

[childhood fragments, part one]

As a child, I'd read with a flashlight under the blanket. My favorite book was *Clarinda*.

It was my mother's book, and then it was my aunt's. Both had written their names inside the book. After the birth of Gabrielle, I gave it to her, and when she could write, she put her name in it right after mine.

Clarinda is a little girl with wispy thin hair and a round face. She was a rebel. Always late, and always wanting to do other and be other than expected. When she left her house, she had to wear a dress, frilly and poufy. And tight shoes. And white gloves. She hated dressing up.

Most of all, Clarinda hated to take baths, until the day she discovered a duckling in her tub. She spoke with him. The duckling had discovered a whirlpool in his pond and had gotten caught in it. Down he had gone, and up he popped in Clarinda's tub.

Clarinda wondered if the reverse would work, so she hopped in, and pulled the plug. Down Clarinda went. Down the duckling went. And out they both popped, into the pond.

This was the start of Clarinda's adventures. This became the life that mattered. She'd visit the duckling. She swam and climbed trees. Her best friend was a little red fox called Freddy.

I wanted to go down the drain and emerge into a pond. Just like Clarinda. Run naked into a pond. Swing on a vine. Live in a tree house.

In my childhood backyard stood a
glorious willow.

I dragged our picnic table under the tree,
pulled the two benches up onto the table top,
and became a castaway on a raft.

The cave of the willow tree was my portal.

Age seven. We move from East Meadow, and I
have to leave the tree. I am bereft. We move to
a house surrounded by oaks, trees that mean
nothing to me. Stiff heavy thick old trees.

My mother tells me that the new owners of our
old house cut down the willow.

I can hardly bear it.

[*guide*]

Winslow schedules a time to visit me at home.
We sit together in the living room. On the couch.
Still, still Steve's chair is in the corner. She lights
a candle. Places a quartz crystal on the
coffee table.

She pulls out her tarot deck. She turns over the
cards and I move through the portal the cards
offer. Something I had never done before,
something I would have judged before,
provided instead a portal.

I am the eight of swords.

I stand in the midst of eight swords.
Blindfolded, bound. Alone. Trapped.

But not really.

The rope binding me is loose. I can remove
the blindfold. I can walk around the swords.

This entrapment is a pause.

I listen. I hear birds.
I smell. I breathe in the scent of flowers
just blossoming.

I am the Hanged Man.

I hang from the beam by one leg. Struggle
creates panic and discomfort. My arms flail
about. Until I settle into the reality, relax into the
discomfort. I will not fall. I am held. It is certainly
not comfortable upside down. But I am held. I
can control my response. Nothing more to do.
Nothing external to me can be controlled.

I begin to see Winslow weekly.

I drive down a tree-lined winding country
road. Entering her house is another threshold
moment. The room we meet in is warmed by the
wood stove and lit by candles. I push aside
a curtain and move into a sacred space.

An oasis.
A place outside of time.
Crystals create an island in the corner of
the room.
Framed as a quest, this journey to
(re)discover connection.

Sometimes in my despair I send a flare in the
guise of a text. In bed at night, in the morning
over coffee, the panic surprises me. And
Winslow responds. Always.

I do not want to see the reality of what I lost. I
ignore and hide the physical reality of Steve's

death. I set aside the rage that the physical absence calls up in me. I focus on the truth that Steve is still present, although unseen.

Driven by forces uncontrollable, the horror panic rage I feel toward the reality that I will never see Steve again as he was drives me deeper into despair.

Agonizing confusion. Homesickness.

Stepping out of panic. Finding something anything to hold onto and stop this free fall, Winslow allows for me to dialogue with myself, and to hear Steve.

Through perspective, movement can occur. The way through is clear. Look up, Beth. Look up.

I begin to learn how to become the hero of my life.

4

waking dream

[a short fairy tale]

There lived a girl. She remembered little outside of the cave. How she arrived there? She could not recall.

The cave was hollow, dark, and very cozy. She had a soft sleeping loft that she had built, or that had been built for her (she wasn't sure, in truth). She would climb up the rickety wooden ladder and crawl onto the platform she rigged up somehow (when? how? unclear, still). There was a blanket. But that was all. An abundance of feathers. And that blanket. A cocoon for sleeping. She'd crawl into the pile of down and immediately move into sleep. Cross into sleep, really. She seemed to notice the shift. The movement from the loft and the feathers and the blanket to the place of jewels and colors, and glistening threads of crystal.

[star]

The Star card from the tarot: I am naked,

kneeling at the edge of a small pool. I hold two

containers of water. One foot is on the ground.

And the other foot in the river. Behind me shines

one large star and seven smaller stars. I need to

open. I need to cleanse. The sacred ibis roosts

in the tree.

[*cave, revisited*]

Cave defined as a noun is an underground chamber. As a verb, it is quite different—and yet absolutely the same. To cave in implies some sort of submission, a surrender. Also, a yielding under pressure. I suppose the pressure can be self-imposed, self-originated. Etymologically? Derived from the Old French, from Latin: *cava*, from *cavus*, meaning hollow. Obsolete, but relevant: it means to excavate, or to hollow out.

To receive, a hollowing need occur. Either passively, or actively.

I have been somewhat obsessively reflecting on caves. Grottos, too.

Surrendering.

[emergence]

Three weeks after Steve's death, I return
to teaching.

I live in a small town in Western Massachusetts
and my drive is twenty minutes up and around
surrounding hills. Every morning I teach I
(grudgingly) wake early, leaving behind the
dream world I am happy in. I make coffee. I light
a candle on the mantle. I sit on my couch, and
write. I dialogue with myself. I dialogue with
Steve. And I feel a sacred something. Curled up,
blanket wrapped around me, I write and think,
and cry.

Until it is time to leave.

Quickly getting dressed, then grabbing my
books, my computer, and a mug of hot coffee,

I head out. And drive to school.

Every day week after week I do this. And every
day week after week I listen to music that makes
me cry while I drive to school. I long for Steve. I
sob. Fred Astaire. Jimmy Durante. Ella and Louis.
All the music that speaks of Steve and of our
relationship plays on shuffle. And for all those
twenty minutes to school I feel bereft.

Sometimes I am so close to despair I think
I will literally break apart. I feel untethered,
uncentered, close to the edge.

Once at school, I set all of that aside. Wash my
face in the bathroom and prepare for the day.

Sometimes I cannot make the shift so gracefully. I
sit in the car trying to breathe.

[—waldo]

It is a warm day, early November. Behind our house is a path that leads to the woods. I rarely walk. But on this day, I walk.

Trees create a canopy, an entrance almost. I am grieving, in such despair. I no longer notice the trees. Or the roots that trip me.

No reason. No logic.
The situation is just is as it is.

And then he is there. Tall. Such heaviness, every footstep seems to take more effort than he is capable of. He doesn't see me.

His six-year-old child has died. His child. The child who would sit under his feet while he wrote. Who would follow him about. Who hunted for mushrooms. And for faeries.

That child. Dead.

Inconsolable, he could find no meaning.

Sir?

He looks down at me. Slow motion. Slow to focus.
Coming from someplace far off.

Then, he speaks.

After my wife's death . . . Ellen's, I mean. I thought
nothing worse could befall me. But this. This is more
than I seem able to bear. And yet it has not touched
me in any way visible.

I remain unmoving. Stunned. Awestruck. Words
fail to speak to the unfathomable nature of this
meeting, and to the abyss of grief this man is lost in.

I am sorry, sir. To lose a child. I am sorry.

Portals of transformation, he continued. Words are needed that might renew, that might create anew. But we are here. Spiritual beings trapped, isolated in physical forms. What a shallow thing grief is.

That is something I understand.

His young son died and the suffering he experiences is not teaching him anything. At least logically, that is. His despair blinds him to the continued presence and comfort that exists along with the suffering.

[hawks redux]

Two months after Steve's death, Ari and Noah are
off to a photo shoot. They had taken over their
father's business. They meet the photographer
in a field. I join them. It is an open vista. I feel
Steve—the glory of the surroundings, our two
sons holding one another and smiling, the sky,
the clouds, the mountains in the distance. I know
there must be a hawk somewhere.

Sometimes this joyful grieving overwhelms. I
leave the shoot, get in the car, close my eyes for
a moment, and the most amazing red fills me.
Then, vibrant purple-tinged red floods my visual
field. I feel comforted, held, joyful.

And sorrowful.

I go home.

Later, Ari says there was a hawk at the shoot. It landed on a tree near us and seemed to watch for the hours we worked. When we left, the hawk left.

The next morning I go to the gym. I step outside for some air and see a hawk hovering. Then, almost without pause, I see three fly off together in one direction and a lone one fly off in the other direction.

Later that day, I pick up Noah from his friend's house. A hawk soars and circles. Noah says the hawk has been there for over an hour.

Be cheerful, Beth.

Our revels now are ended. These our actors,
As I foretold you, were all spirits and
Are melted into air, into thin air.

Shakespeare,
The Tempest

[*—paradox, continued*]

Shakespeare,
King Lear

I'd crack heaven wide open with my laments.
Gone forever. He is gone. Forever.

But I am not Lear carrying his dead child. I do
not howl. At least not audibly. I am moving deep
within. To a place others cannot hear. Others
cannot see.

A howl muted. An inarticulate cry of utter
anguish. Beyond above below words. The sound
an animal makes. The sound of a powerful gale.
A natural sound. A human sound. But muted.
And agonizing.

[howl heard]

It is a calm night. In a place without any
electricity. The stars brilliantly above clearly seen.
The walk to the lodge accompanied by others.
Bare feet on warm sand. Pausing outside the
entrance. Needing to crouch down and crawl
into the narrow tunnel marking the entrance.

Months after Steve's death I am in a sweat lodge
in Mexico, and it is there in the womblike safety
of the lodge that I howl audibly. Among women
I have grown to love and trust, guided by a
shaman, I experience the darkness that the
howl marked.

It is a primordial cry of complete despair
and loss.

That howl marks the place of meaninglessness.

It marks regret for all the wasted hours.

Call me, a friend had written. And you can rage.
With me. In safety.

And I thought, why? I don't feel anger. Despair?
Yes. Sadness. But not anger.

But just because I did not experience or see or
acknowledge anger, does not mean that anger
did not exist.

I think now that I was afraid of my anger. Of the
force of my rage.

Anger derives from Old Norse *angr*, meaning
grief, or *angra vex*.

Anger and grief. Assuredly inextricably linked.

And regret? Regret derives from bewailing the dead. To bewail. The dead.

[chaos]

Chaos. Unknowing. Resting in the uncertainty.
Holding two opposing points and remaining
content with something essentially unresolvable.

I tremble on the precipice of the inner abyss.

I am thrust into chaos. Nothing makes sense. I
am unmoored. Lost. This cannot be.

Logic cuts. It dissects. It analyzes. It distances the
subject (me) from the (desired) object (Steve).
But by quieting the brain, a way out or a way
through is possible. The binary is a trap. Polarities
exist, but either extreme results in a disconnect
of some sort. Life requires movement and
change. Stasis is death.

I live in a liminal space. Simultaneously existing

in the past and in the (paradoxical

shocking undigestible joyful magical

inconceivable) present.

I look to be in the now, to open to what is

rather than long for what is not and what

cannot be.

It is not possible through logic nor, in truth,

through feeling. It is possible, though.

The night Steve died is the night I moved into

another realm. A boundless boundary-less

fluid space. The liminal.

[dream]

Gabrielle dreamed:

A group of women walk to a mountain. The mountain is alive with colors—green, red-orange, gold, pink, and a sand-colored pigment.

A hawk soars above. Huge. A white chest, brown feathers. All clearly visible.

Our friends guide Gabrielle and me down a road over a small bridge to the destination.

That mountain.

Gabrielle says there are either four or seven women. She is unsure.

They give us a tour.

We see animals. Flowers. The colors are ridge-
like. Textured.

Gabrielle looks up and sees the white-bellied
hawk moving directly above her head, soaring
over the colors of the mountain.

There is a hut built from pine.

I want to go in. We read the sign, note the rules.
I go forward. Alone into the hut.

[howl heard, part two]

I go to Mexico to experience the sorrow that is drowning me. The land can absorb my tears. So I am told. The land can absorb the tears that can no longer be held back. And that I cannot permit myself to move into while with my children.

I go knowing that my friend will be there by my side.

We go into the sweat lodge. Mary offers to act as my guide.

Sacred.

Horrifying.

Women howling. Heat. Thick air. I can't breathe. I can't sing. And finally. Eventually. With

trepidation. With the wish to not say it, I do.
Over and over.

No.

No.

No.

No.

No.

I don't like this. Come back. Come back. I don't
like this.

I howl. For the first time. Deep. Guttural. I go as
far as I can. I see the abyss. I cannot find a place
to hold onto.

But then, I do. I find connection. I find breath.

I am not alone.
Not really.

Through the steam I feel Mary's hand.

Mary's arm.

Loving.

The mother.

Comforting. Loving.

And then it is over.

Mary is in front of me. We crawl blindly through
the steam-filled lodge, our path marks a circle.
We crawl through the narrow tunnel that
leads out.

Dante,
Inferno XXXIV
To get back up to the shining world

from there

My guide and I went into that

hidden tunnel,

And following its path, we took no care

To rest, but climbed: he first, then I—so far,

through a round aperture I saw appear

Some of the beautiful things that
  Heaven bears,
Where we came forth, and once more
  saw the stars.

[-The dollhouse]

I am thirteen. I become a Bat Mitzvah. I take my
gift money and buy a dollhouse.

Three stories. Swiss chalet. The furniture was
hand painted. Bright blue beds with white
flowers. Fluffy down-filled mattresses. Red and
white checked. The windows had blue curtains.
A kitchen with a white table and tiny wooden
chairs, red backed, white flowers painted on the
seat backs. A living room with a wood stove. I
had never seen one before. The kind of stove a
family would sit around.

I purchase a family of dolls. A mother. A father. A
sister. A brother. And a baby.

I love that family. Although I rarely play with the
mother and the father.

I am thirteen and my mother and my family think
it funny that I would want something like this
as a teenager. I put my dollhouse into my large
closet. Darkling, in that closet, I play with
my dolls.

And outside that closet door?

My bedroom. A mass of bright pink carpeting
and loud patterned bedding. A television, a
stereo. A telephone.

And beyond that bedroom?
My house. Television sets blaring. Phones
ringing. Slamming doors.
People fighting.

Burdened by a life built on a foundation

(paradoxically) illusory. Appearances. Surfaces.

Alienated and isolated.

I fragment myself.

[present child]

Grandma loves pussy willows. She seems always to have some in a vase. The willows are so soft.

Still, still I can hear grandma sitting at her upright piano, singing.

There is a picture of me at age three or four. I wear a pink one-piece bathing suit. My hair is golden from the sun. I stand at the top of the highest metal slide. My hands are above my head, holding onto the bar above. I am absolutely completely solidly present. Fearless. Chubby legs. Belly protruding slightly. Eyes open. I gaze upward.

The metal ladder is hot on my bare feet. Children struggle to climb. Parents put their hands on the railing of the ladder to protect their children.

I scamper up. Alone. I love scaring myself
physically. The slide was for the big children
and I am far from big. But down I go. I love
the speed.

I spend many days at that beach club in Point
Lookout. You have a cabana, Grandma. You and
your lady friends play Mah-Jongg. I hear the
clicking of the tiles on the metal card table. I
watch you drink your iced tea. And laugh. You set
the table near the cabanas, four chairs around
it. Your cabana includes a small shower stall and
a dressing area. You have Cashmere Bouquet
talcum powder. The powder comes in a metal
tin. It smells of flowers. It smells of you.

I spend my days in the pool, or on the swings
and the slides, or digging in the sand, and when
it is almost time to leave and the sun is just a bit
lower over the ocean, and the sand is just a bit

colder on my feet, I shower in your cabana. The sand that is caught in all the crevices of my body is washed off, and pools in the cement floor of the shower, eventually swirling down the drain.

After my shower, you come into the stall and powder me.

As often as I can, I visit you and Grandpa in Long Beach. The silences in your house a balm.
A pause. An oasis.

You live a few blocks in from the boardwalk.
I reach up and hold Grandpa's hand. You cannot walk on the sand, but wait for us on the boardwalk.

You watch over us.

It is dark under the boardwalk. I take off my

shoes and feel the cool sand on my feet. I hold my bucket in one hand. And Grandpa holds my other. Light manages to find its way through the slats above.

When we step out from under the boardwalk the sand shifts from cool to warm. Okay, Grandpa says. Off you go. I run to the edge of the sea. And the sand changes again. Moist. Cool. I dig moats. Build my castle. I invite the water to fill my moat. I fill the bucket with water. Then pour the water into the moat. The water remains pooled for a moment. Then the sand drinks it all up.

[present self]

This whole experience of re/membering.

Putting my self together. It's overflowing with

ambiguities, unanswerables.

Now shedding layers willingly, or by force. I

stand exposed.

I stand as Beth.

[art]

Gabrielle paints a small canvas the winter
following her father's death. Red. Violent. Painted
on and woven in the bloody painting are sparks
of white light fractured and jagged. A street light
shines through dense fog. In the chaos of the
painting I experience an underlying sense of
shock and transformation.

At a gallery opening, I stand unmoving in front of
the painting. Then walk outside into the hallway
and collapse against the wall.

I buy the painting.

[—the body]

Ed told me about the Jewish ritual for burial.
Hevra Kadesha. Ritual burial. I had never heard
of such a thing.

The trauma that you experienced. The accident
itself. The people gaping at you in your final
moments alive. The autopsy. All of this needed
to be purified somehow. And so when Ed
mentioned this, I said yes. Without knowing what
it involved. Without hesitation.

I wish I could have been the one to tend to you.

I asked myself if I could wash your body. Look
at the injuries without any lighting or padding
masking what you experienced.

I could not.

After your burial, I dream. I experience the
ritual. I am with you. I am you. I do not see what
is being done to you/me, but I experience/
feel/know the care. And I see the friends that
selflessly and without expectation of thanks
perform the ritual.

I am naked. I am bruised. Dishonored. And with
love I am purified. Healed. I am washed. Each leg
is lifted and washed and oiled. And prayed over.
Each arm. The torso. My head. I cannot move,
but receive.

And release.

And then I see. And I know that death is a birth.

The wrapping of the body in the white shroud is
not something I dreamed. But it is what I know
was done.

You were prepared to return. To be placed in the earth.

A statement of gratitude for the body that housed you.

A birth.

The ritual cleansing.

Your body is wrapped in a white shroud.

You are placed in the casket.

The casket is placed in the room.

The top of the casket is closed.

We sit with you during the night before the burial.

Gabrielle.

Ari.

Noah.

Me.

And friends.

And during those hours we read to you, or speak
to you.

I speak to you.

You are never alone.

5

the albatross

[you saved me, yet unawares, part first]

It's time to release the albatross. But to do that I
need to bless my self. To dialogue with my self.
As you did.

As you do.

[-unnameable]

Beth,

It was in Paris. When you were nineteen, almost
twenty years old, five days before you met A.,
you sat outside of Sacre Coeur on the steps,
and read poetry: Keats. You were drowning in
sounds, baffling, incomprehensible, seemingly
untranslatable. You held the book in your hands
and turned the pages. There. You read. Tender,
precise, rigorous lines that moved through
your being.

When A. looked at you over thirty years ago
(that other life) across a small table in that cafe,
he said you were beautiful, and he meant it.
That really might have been the moment: seen.
Any perplexing/retarding/cautionary thoughts
discarded.

You open the book. The binding is broken. The cover is worn. Your version of the sacrament: baguette and espresso. And Keats.

You turn the pages. There. You allow the words to permeate. *My heart aches and a drowsy numbness pains/My sense, as though of hemlock I had drunk...*

Can it all be attributed to youth? (The impulsivity, the desperation, the lack of any sense of consequence?) Ignorance? To a degree. Perhaps.

Back home. NYC. You and A. had been home from Paris for less than a week. Your mother drove you to the hospital. She helped check you in. You were given a room. A hospital gown. Then you were put to sleep. No one named the reason for your admittance. (Does that not naming make it not real? You wonder about that now.)

And when you woke? A. was there. He had flowers. You were happy to see him. Neither of you needed to speak.

Your father arrived. He looked at A. with disdain, could barely frame the question —How can you be here?

The response? Silence.

You looked at A. At the flowers. A. glanced at you, but briefly. He put the flowers on the table by the door.

And then? He left.

Days later. Not quite a week after you were in the hospital. Not quite a week after A. left. Not quite a week after. You began to bleed—heavily. You were told this might happen, so you ignored the blood. You took the subway uptown. Went to class: Russian Lit, of course. Dostoevsky.

But then you felt cramping—severe. You thought, I deserve this. I need to suffer, but the pain and the bleeding became too severe to ignore. You went home to the apartment that you shared with your aunt.

You phoned A. What do you want from me? he said. He hung up. You never spoke again.

You went out. You hailed a cab. You went to the hospital alone. You needed another procedure, an emergency procedure. An incomplete abortion? This time, no one would know. This time you were awake. This time you heard the sounds. You knew you were being emptied, scraped clean is what you thought.

No room.

No gown.

No family.

[. . .]

No flowers.

[*life*]

A month later you met Steve.

[excavation]

The etymology of excavate is to hollow out.

Excavation both metaphorical and tangible.

The incomplete abortion that sent me to the
emergency room. This required an excavation.
One that I was fully conscious during.

Excavating to discover the Beth hiding.

Excavating to learn to know the Beth that
Steve loved.

[you saved me, yet unawares, part the second]

Steve saved me. And he offered the way to save myself. Unawares?
Not really.

Here. Now. I need to discover the beauty in the lowest and darkest and most shameful-feeling part of my life. Or, at least let a little light in. I need to crawl out of the grotto, and stand up.

6

dead

There are more things in heaven and Earth, Horatio,

Than are dreamt of in your philosophy

[*sideways into the liminal*]

When the officer asked who I wanted to call to
be with me, I answered, you. Of course, you. You.
Always you. From the first, we established this—if
I needed help of any sort, I called you.

How crazy to remember that night thirty years
ago in my apartment on Amsterdam Avenue. We
were friends. Not lovers. Not yet. The fuse blew. I
was having a bit of a moment with a date. On the
couch. But when the lights blew, I called you.

And you came.
And you fixed the fuse.
While I sat on the couch with my date.
And I wondered.

So, in this new state. This sideways move? I
was with you. As you were in the process of

becoming. Not material physical Steve, but still
you. Metamorphosed. And with you I was okay.
Really okay. In that space, it all made sense. It
was sad not to have you here physically.
But I was clearly with you.

Still. Still.

Always.

It took two days from the time of the accident for
the hospital to release you to the funeral parlor.

Until your body was close to home—sideways
into panic.

Where are you?

I didn't ask to see you in the morgue.
I didn't ask to be taken to you that night

you died.

I didn't wonder about that then. But I
wonder now.

I took care of your physical body. I arranged for
the ritual care required. I sat with you. I held your
hand. I saw you leave your body when we were
in the room with you. I saw you smile.

By attention to detail. By caring for you,
physically and spiritually, I remained okay.
Sort of okay. Not completely okay. But okay
enough. Considering.

In those early days? I danced to "Cheek to
Cheek." Alone in the living room, I danced
alone. I pulled out the recording of Astaire and
I danced. I closed my eyes and imagined you
holding me. My right hand resting in yours. Your
arm gently around my waist.

And I swayed to the music. With you. And I felt
you. And was comforted.

And sobbing.

Grief doesn't mark us in any obvious way.

> *Heavenly Hurt, it gives us –*   Dickinson
> *We can find no scar,*
> *But internal difference –*
> *Where the Meanings, are –*

Internal difference. Silences. Voids. The space
where the connection is recognized, re/
cognized. Re/thought.

And re/membering can happen.

[regret]

Sleepwalking years. That's what I call them. Of course that's not what I thought they were when I lived them. I thought myself awake.

But I wasn't awake. I wasn't awake to the man I lived with. I rarely looked at you. I wasn't seeing.

I saw after you died. After you left. And after you returned.

But that moment. Your departure. Reaching out toward you. Yearning. Desperate. No. No. Don't leave. Just at the moment I see you.

The ache is different now. I'm not drowning.

But the missing continues.

And the regret.

[pearls]

Loneliness while sharing a life.

Thirty years with another person requires
movement. Maturation on the part of the
individuals does not always result in
constant harmony.

To put it mildly.

Both of us experienced this.

We created separate lives. Parallel lives.
Independent. Supportive in unspoken ways.

I remember people's surprise when they realized
we were married. That's how separately we lived.

An abyss between us.

For a time.

Driving home from school. Pulling into the
driveway. Getting out of the car. Seeing the
front door open, and you and our dog bursting
out of the doorway, joyfully running toward me.
Greeting me. Both wagging your tails.

And my response? Impatience. How silly I
thought you were.
This greeting irritated me no end.
This greeting was a regular occurrence.
Daily, in fact.
As was my reaction. A regular occurrence,
I mean.
And, yes, daily.

I imagined my life with a tall dark
handsome knight.
I imagined my hero greeting me with
a bottle of wine.

I imagined candlelit dinners and conversations about Kierkegaard and Keats.

I was with a man who played honky-tonk on the piano.
A man who modeled his greeting on our dog.
A man who offered me green juice and crystals.

When I pull into my driveway now and the front door doesn't open, and no one runs out to greet me, I realize I had been married to my knight after all.

[_light_]

I watch the video of our city wedding. Ari and
Noah. And me. We watch. And there is a moment
when I feel physically ill because I see. Transient.
Ephemeral. The observable ease with which
we move. Light and loving. Clear love. My arms
around your neck. Kissing you. Hugging you.

And I think: She is so young. Even her voice
is higher. There's no depth to it. This young
woman is a girl.

I see you reach out and put your hand on my
hat. (We were married on the rooftop of the
restaurant.) It is a windy day. When the wind
picked up and the hat was more of a nuisance
than an enhancement, I take it off and shake my
head. Gaze up at the sun. For just a moment.

I feel beautiful. And loved. I am giddy, buoyant. Laughing. Unable to be still.

And Steve? You. Zeppo to my Groucho. And then there was "Cheek to Cheek." And Steve and Beth danced. They held one another easily. Tenderly.

In the sanctuary at the funeral service, again "Cheek to Cheek." I forgot the enormity of the love that the song offered. I melted into Steve's arms. Then. And during that other then.

Now? The end of something real and good and right. And whole. And primarily previously unseen unrecognized. The continuation of the essence of what was there.

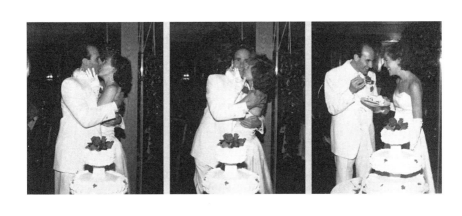

[*dancing in the liminal*]

The air is thick. Not thick like it was on the night
you died. Or like the night the branch from the
white beech tree shattered a window on the
front porch. Thick with beings. With substance
that is unearthly unairlike.

There is so much happening outside of the
funeral service. A river of people. Filling the
sanctuary. Overflowing. One thousand people.
The rabbis speak. People pray. I speak. Gabrielle
speaks. Ari speaks. Noah speaks. We are held by
you. Your arms embrace us. Rick and Joel speak,
standing slightly apart from one another, as if
holding the space for you. Michael speaks.

There is a sense of cushioning. Gentle muffling,
almost. Like being surrounded by cotton balls.

Ari said many months later that he wondered why he was in the back of the sanctuary and not seated with us.

But you were with us, I answer.

We move in and out, between realms. Wide awake and completely asleep. We are both in a vision and in a waking dream.

And then I feel myself smiling. And wanting to laugh. Not hysteria. Joy. Because I am with Steve. He is there with us. And in an understanding deeper than words I know we are okay. We are all okay. And we would be okay. And so is Steve. And so would Steve be.

Our friend plays the song at the funeral. The song we danced to at our wedding. The song that always made us smile, that made us stop bickering. The song that made us look at one another, smile, reach out our arms toward one another, and laugh, and dance. Just that. Dance. Hold one another. And love one another. No words. Nothing more. Just the song taking us out of our daily life and providing a path toward (re)connection.

When Steve was alive. This was so.

Why wouldn't something similar happen at the funeral? A shedding of the physical, a movement to a different plane. That's all death is.

When we went to see Steve after the accident in the funeral home he seemed to be holding himself together. He looked stern. Uncomfortable. But then we surrounded him. All of us. The children. His brothers. My dear friend. That's when I saw an exhale of sorts. I saw Steve relax. And then—crazily—he smiled. Did you see that? And then, in answer, he smiled again. I held his hand. I rubbed his arm. You always hated when I rubbed your arm like this, I said, but now I can do it without any griping. And then? Steve released himself from his body. He moved away from it.

So, at the funeral? The music provides a space where I meet Steve, and we dance, and I sing. Did I sing out loud? I don't really know. But I feel as if I did. And I feel myself swaying and smiling and dancing and singing with Steve, for Steve, in honor of my husband.

And after the service when we all walk out, I am very much between realms and I am smiling, feeling so light and joyous. And we drive to the cemetery. At the cemetery, I help carry the casket. I need to carry the casket. And as we sit by the hole that would receive Steve I feel the rightness of this ceremony. I feel strongly that the earth would hold Steve.

And it was good.
And when we shovel dirt onto the lowered casket I feel strangely empowered and I want to fill the hole myself.

The sound of the dirt hitting the casket, the sound that I had always hated, is a sound that provides comfort. Because Steve's physical body is safe. And honored. The sound of the dirt hitting the wooden casket is like a gentle rain that slowly and steadily nourishes the tender buds.

The hundreds of mourners create a pathway for us to walk through after the burial. I look down this pathway and feel overwhelmed. Students.

Members of our temple. Cousins. Aunts and uncles. Friends. How would the children and I ever walk past so many people? But when we step into this created path I feel transported yet again. This pathway is created by love. And such a love pouring forth from so many people that it becomes a force, it has a substance to it that carries us. And I walk and smile, and nod.

And when I am halfway someone says, The planes. Steve's pilot buddies are doing a fly over in honor of Steve. And with that first shout I look up and someone says, A hawk! Out of nowhere appears a red-tailed hawk. It flies in formation with the planes, maintaining appropriate distance from the other planes. The hawk flies with the planes. This is a very unhawklike thing, of course.

And it is at this point that even the most cynical

say, That's Steve! Because it is.

And at that moment, I am transported yet again,
this time straight up. And there I meet Steve
again, and we dance.

Again.

7
connection

Honore
de Balzac
Death unites as well as separates; it silences all paltry feeling.

[*already with thee*]

I live in the liminal.

I am neither fully in the now, lost in the past,
or looking ahead. I'm moving between.
Perpetually moving.

It's a space that I've never consciously been in
before. A space without boundaries. There's
no heaven above and hell below. At least not
as far as I can discern. As far as I can tease out,
it's really all on the same plane and is, rather,
a matter of perception. It's an ability to move
between, to listen intuitively with the right brain.
To feel the warmth and joy that is Steve.

Liminal is derived from the Latin *limen*, meaning
threshold. It is a transitional or initial stage of a
process. It means a position in more than one

realm. Or, in a sense, in no realm. Pure potential.

Limitless energy. It recognizes boundaries,

and yet exists in the boundless. It is sometimes

concluded to be the realm of the imagination. I

experience it as a reality, almost tangible.

On the night of Steve's death I was thrust into a

realm I had previously intellectualized but was

now forced to live in.

[learning to read]

Music bypasses the intellect that stops
connection. It reaches me through the heart. It's
the consciousness that poetry aspires to inspire.
The bridge, really. The songs I hear act as portals.
They are my version of the tarot. I move into the
song and let it fill me. And I feel connection. And
"Cheek to Cheek" still brings me immediately
to Steve, and–I suppose–brings him to me. Our
way of flagging one another.

[present longing]

Noah dreamed of Steve.

In the dream Noah watches a show, and in
the show someone dies. The actors show the
audience the dead body.

Noah says, I've seen a dead body.

Noah says, In the show the person wasn't really
dead even though they saw the dead body.

Noah says to me, I had a hard day today.

[*visits*]

Noah dreamed of Steve. He is with his father. Steve tells him that he was dead, but he's not now. They talk and work out details about the Sproutman business, discussing manufacturers and contacts.

Then Steve says he has to be dead again.

Noah wakes happy.

Ari dreamed of Steve. He is with his father. Steve walks up the driveway. Ari greets him, asks how Steve could be there.

You're dead, aren't you? We had a funeral. We got insurance money.

Steve keeps repeating, It's all right, Ari. It's all right. Ari takes him up to the newly organized office.

Ari says he was afraid what his father would say. After all, he'd been through Steve's stuff, rearranged the office, etc.

Steve says, It's all right, Ari. He gives Ari his wallet, says he put money into it.

Ari wakes happy.

Noah dreamed of Steve.
They talk business.
Dreaming Noah says, I need to remember to tell Mommy.

Noah dreamed of Steve.
They are in the kitchen. Steve cleans the sprouter. They discuss where to order seeds.

Noah wakes happy.
Ari wakes with a start this morning.

Hears Steve say, Sheena vaka?

A nonsensical phrase that we used.

Noah dreamed of Steve. He flies with his
father. We thought you were dead, he says.
But here you are.

Gabrielle dreamed of Steve. I thought you
were dead, she says.

I dreamed of Steve.

He is not dead. There was a mistake.

Someone else was buried.

I see Steve at a theatre. He looks wonderful.

Is wearing his hat.

But he is not flexible, soft, living.

We speak.

He is bigger than in life. Stronger. Very upright.

His skin has an almost porcelain quality.

Shimmering. He is not warm, but cold, like he

was when I held him after he had died.

He is very present. And very real.

Who did I bury?, I keep repeating.

I wake happy.

The morning after the dream a beautiful cardinal

sits in the small tree in the front yard.

[unveiling]

September 2016.

One year later. At the gravesite.

The rabbi removes the cloth that covers your stone. Everyone laughs.

I wanted a stone that was ethereal, that defied the physical. I thought of Michelangelo. I thought of Rodin. I wanted a stone that gave the feeling of soaring. Of light. Of metamorphosis.

As Ari and Noah and Gabrielle and I stood with the woman who would make the stone I said, we need to write something about love. Because that's what Steve was all about, really. Love. It needs to be an active statement. An expression of movement.

Not only the word loving.

Something, though.

And then I heard, Choose Love.

Choose Love, I said.

And with that, I felt a huge rush of presence. Of acknowledgment. Of joy.

Yes, the children agreed. Definitely that.

And more, I said. We should have one of daddy's sprout drawings on the stone.

The illustrations that Steve had in his books and in his early promotional materials were cartoons that his friend, Michael Parman had done. Michael died a number of years before Steve.

It seemed more than fitting to have Michael's illustration on Steve's stone.

Choose Love.

[*prometheus, a vision*]

Gabrielle dreamed. She is bound and tethered
to a crag. Put in a harness. Then Steve arrives,
like a crow. Or, a blackbird. He moves slowly,
gently. She tries to imitate his movements but is
unable because she is bound. But she imagines
flying with him. Longs to fly with him.

Then, sudden metamorphosis. He grows larger.
Elongated. His face begins to change from a
bird's into his human form. But he still has
wings and when he moves his wings, she
sees every feather.

[prometheus, unbound]

Absence does not mean non-existence.

Rather, absence implies presence. Or, eventual

presence. An empty pitcher is waiting to be

filled with some delicious liquid, or some wild

flowers. To be able to receive is what is possible

when one is filled with the negative. But it

requires surrender. A quieting of the brain which

perplexes and retards, and stops me from seeing

that I am already with Steve.

But negative has another meaning with a

more overtly moral connotation—opposition.

To be negative implies a closing off or a self-

imprisonment, often with an accompanying

feeling of despair or hopelessness.

This is the paradox of death. Presence and

absence. Reaching out and trying to touch

what cannot be touched. Sitting in silence and experiencing presence.

Was I robbed? Am I a passive victim in this life?

I don't feel that.

I feel I was gifted and that I am gifted.

I travel in realms I don't understand and see threads of glistening strands. I am in a matrix of unintelligible something. An unmarked place that forbids orientation and halts meaning. I have had an almost apocalyptic experience, but know somehow that this apparently fragmented world will eventually return to an undivided condition. I hold to this: everything is essentially interconnected.

And there is a way to read this through a right

understanding of the signs that are somehow illuminating my path like lanterns placed in an otherwise black landscape.

[Theatre]

In one of the last pictures I took of you, if not
the last, you are in the theatre. We went to a
production of "His Girl Friday. " You had made
a donation to the local public radio station and
won the incentive, two tickets.

"His Girl Friday" was an end of summer
production. You were happy to take me out,
and I was happy to go.

I had returned a week or so before from my
summer residency. Something had shifted,
settled between us. I enjoyed your company in
a way that I had not for many years. I suspect the
same was true for you.

I was in Vermont. You came up for a couple
of nights.

You sat on a couch and I was on another. I looked at you and felt such enormous gratitude for you. You weren't doing anything, really. Just sitting, working on some business project. But we were together.

And I thought how wondrous to be able to just be.
We didn't speak.
It was quiet.

The apartment I rented was a garage apartment, set back from a road dominated by farms. I was studying Milton and Borges and Calvino that summer. My books were in piles on the coffee table. On the nightstand. And on the shelf above my desk. I was able to spend my days reading and writing, and studying. Attending classes that excited me. I felt a huge exhale that summer. Even the stress of composing work that satisfied was oddly healing.

And you were visiting. And all I needed to do with you was be.

And then, on the beach. We were more attuned to one another than we'd been in decades. Lying on the beach, I curled up next to you. Your chest was warm. I curled up under your arm, my arm across your chest.

I was falling in love. Again.

It was a moment outside of time. And it was like that for me when it was happening. I was cushioned somehow. Aware of the enormity and the miracle. You asleep on your back on a rocky beach on Block Island. Ari and Noah riding a moped around the island, exploring. And me? No book, just you. My hand on your warm chest.

The fragility of everything oddly present.

And now I was home, and we were going
to a play.

You always said you were born too late—you
loved the 1940s. Ella. Durante. Uncle Milty. This
show? Your kind of show. We'd seen the Cary
Grant and Rosalind Russell film more than once.
That patter they could do! The gaffes, the missed
opportunities, the bickering. And the eventual
union at the end. The mismatched lovers
rediscovering they were better together. And
throughout? Laughter. Lots and lots of laughter.

Before and after the happily ever after.

Look at the set!, you said. Like a kid in
that theatre.

You read the program cover to cover.

Before the show, we had dinner at Baba Louie's—
gourmet pizza, a glass of wine for me. Then the
show. A good night.

Hello Hildy, he called out gleefully.
Hello Walt, she answered with a sly smile.

We knew what was coming.

We knew the struggle ahead.

And we loved every minute.

[*flying*]

In the therapist's office. Twenty years into
our marriage.

What excites you about Steve, the
therapist asked.

His mastery, I answered without hesitation.

And where do you see that?

When he plays piano. When he flies. He flies like
a musician. Feeling the currents of air. Knowing
how to have that machine respond to his gentle
but knowing touch. That look of mastery, of
peace that he has when he flies. That excites me.

And?

Yes, it seems I should fly, I answered.

And?

I tried.

I closed my eyes as you revved the engine. I kept my eyes closed as we picked up speed. They remained closed until this moment of suddenly breaking free from the force that holds us to the earth. It's a specific moment. There's tremendous resistance. And then freedom. I don't believe I ever told you this. I loved watching you control the plane. I loved looking out the windows.

So?

If it were turbulent, at all, I'd shift from peace to panic. Just like that. Instant. I'd think we'd crash. And die.

If anyone asked, I'd say I was not a great flyer.

I don't mind heights. And once we were up,
I almost kind of sort of liked it. A lot. But the
anticipation caused such enormous waves of
anxiety, that I rarely joined you.

Which was unfortunate. Which is unfortunate.
And which does cause me regret.

Because when we did fly and the flight was a
smooth one, I would look over at you and be
astonished at the mastery with which you flew.
And the joy that it gave you. Both the flight itself,
I mean, and the fact that you were taking me on
an adventure.

You spoke frequently in the early years about
flights to small islands off of Florida. Pilots'
places. Islands only accessible by small plane, or

boat. Affordable vacations, you'd say. And you'd show me links. Look, you'd say. A Buddy place! Peaceful. Beaches. Quiet. You'll love it, you'd say. And it'd only take us eight hours, maybe nine. And we could land when we need to, you'd say.

And the idea of being almost on a desert island did appeal. But the wave of panic that the actual flight brought up for me was something I could not get through.

And that makes me sad to recall.

Gabrielle was euphoric in the plane. Always. A joyous enthusiastic passenger. Ari and Noah wanted to pilot. And you taught them. Hours and days and weeks and months you spent with them up in the air. And they learned to fly as easily as they walk. They are both skilled pilots. And when you first died, Ari found peace and connection with you through flight.

It's this bird's eye view, you'd say. You loved the perspective. The freedom from the weightiness of life.

I am sorry I couldn't fly with you more than I did. I know you didn't resent this.

But I am sorry nonetheless.

8

both

[*visits*, *continued*]

In the early weeks following Steve's death I am
perpetually gifted with visions. I am offered
Steve's hand and shown the forms and colors
that exist just beneath the visible world.

Clouds, blue, gem-like, crevices, movement.
Blue light radiating like flowers blossoming.
Fireworks of color exploding.
Streaming, coursing forms.

And this:
A figure in the distance stands in some sort of
entryway. The color a golden red. The figure is
dark, seemingly in shadow, but light sparks from
the entryway.

And this:
Flowers bursting and morphing.

Birds, mountains, a craggy place. Distance.

Swirling forms.

A mountain appears. I climb, seeking footholds.

Faces.

Hands.

Beckoning.

Inviting.

Rivers of people. Never still. Never resting.

And then one night lying in bed, trying to settle
in, to breathe, to settle, and not panic, I see a
column of light. Shimmering, glistening light.
A light not of this world. I close my eyes and
still see the column. I open my eyes. The
column remains.

I see Steve.

And another night, threads of glistening light
act almost like a web, interconnected. I open my

eyes. The web. I close my eyes. Still I see.

I get out of bed, I walk through the light.

[—paradox, continued]

Be in the world but not of the world. At least not only. Living something beyond words. How do I explain the bliss? How do I speak to the joy in this apparent horror? In the days after Steve's death I felt cocooned. Shock, I suppose. But more than shock, too. A hum. Tingling. Immense bliss.

I craft an ode to Steve.

I am validated through what I am beginning to call "my poets." Both receiver and giver. It is as you write, Mr. Keats. Your words strike me as my own thoughts and—oddly—as a remembrance. When I read and reread your "Ode to a Nightingale" I have a visceral response. The words take me out of my (limiting) self and into the realm of the other.

I am certain of nothing but of the holiness of the Heart's affections and the truth of Imagination.
(Keats)

[*Keats in the Liminal*]

A restless night. Unable to sleep. Uncomfortable.
Yearning for what is not. Holding on to what is.
To what might be.

I must have slept briefly.

Because when I opened my eyes, Keats was
there, sitting on the window seat. Slight of build.
I knew he was short—only five feet—but he was
more faery-like than I'd expected.

My excitement overwhelmed. My awe
stopped speech.

He was sad. Tender. Seemed to be longing.

No words. From either of us.

I looked away for a moment. Dear young poet,
I thought.

Then, he was gone.

[*negative capability*]

I cannot sleep those first nights after Steve died.
On the first night Noah comes into our bed and
we remain in bed together, not sleeping, not
talking. Just floating, almost.

Too filled with despair to even cry.

On the third night, I am given a sleeping pill.
It puts me to sleep. But it is a dark troubled
sleep. And I wake bereft. Empty. I take another
pill the next night. And wake feeling the same
emptiness. They are static-creating, mind
numbing, deadening. Make otherworldly visions
impossible. They cut me off from the liminal.
Waking from them is annihilating. Absent of
possibility. So, no more pills.

[*imagination*]

I look forward to sleep. To diving into the space where I find Steve.

Imagination. As a state of potential. Of possible metamorphosis. Not a static place, but one humming, twinkling, glittering. A place of creation. Of movement.

I long to reconnect with something foundational. I want to escape the binary.

Dive. Then surface. And retain what has been gifted. But gifted through an active striving.

Truth that is deeper than words. Knowing without the brain. Feeling without the heart.

Words are mere markers. Words are (possible) portals.

Language limits and frees by naming. It defines. Organizes. Catalogues.

Can you catalogue the self? Is it limiting, or freeing?

I am Beth

I am a widow

I am a wife

I am beloved

I am happy

I am sad

I am a mother

I am a writer

I am blessed

I am loved

I am bursting with possibility

I am sad

I am alone

I am surrounded

I am vulnerable

I am entering the ninth month

I am birthing my self

I am reeling

I am blind

I am clear eyed

I am in shock

I am asleep

I am awake

Think without the brain. See without the eyes.

The dance of life is a dance. Particles move
together creating new universes, break apart,
fragment, move.

When I try to reason through this loss, I feel
only despair, but when I feel my way, I can
acknowledge not knowing why and not finding
any reason that is attainable through ordinary
thinking. I can find my way into this raw place

and feel love.

Grief levels, equalizes.

Random thoughts memories poems lines

from books ideas.

All dialogue.

[a (liminal) encounter : whitman]

He is old when he visits me. Unkempt. Untidy.
I can smell him. His hands are gnarled, stained
with ink.

He gazes at me. He sees me. He reaches out his
arms. And I am held. And comforted.

> *They are alive and well somewhere;*   Whitman
> *The smallest sprout shows there is really*
>   *no death,*
> *And if ever there was it led forward life,*
> *and does not wait at the end to arrest it,*
> *And ceased the moment life appeared.*
>
> *All goes onward and outward . . . and*
>   *nothing collapses,*
> *And to die is different from what any one*
>   *supposed, and luckier.*

Everything is in flux. Anything fixed is dead. Like Steve's corpse. Unmoving. Heavy. But transformation, metamorphosis exists.

> *Logic and sermons never convince,*
> *The damp of the night drives deeper*
> *into my soul.*

9

through the looking glass

[alice]

I had a vision two weeks before Steve's death.

We are leaving a gypsy caravan. Old and rickety, it is set up off the ground on wooden stakes. We can enter and exit by walking up or down three steps. There is no door, but a heavy red velvet curtain acts as one. It can be held back with a rope. We speak with the old woman who I know to be a fortune teller. She is helped down the stairs by a young child.

I can communicate with those who have crossed, the old woman says.

Can you help me speak with my stepfather? I ask.

He's right behind you, she says.

I turn to look. Steve is behind me, yet I cannot see him. But I do see a grayish figure, stern, and somewhat forbidding, far in the distant. My stepfather, Andy.

This is not the way, the figure says.

The old woman gestures us to follow her back into the caravan. The four of us sit in a circle. I can see everyone except for Steve. He is present, but not visible.

As soon as the circle is formed, the four of us in our places, and the curtain drawn, a tremendous energy surges through, a whoosh. The most exceptional glorious column of light materializes in the center of our circle.
A pillar. Opaline. Translucent.

A voice speaks from this column. The child

understands and we all understand through the child.

If you knew how beautiful it was on the other side, you would not be sad.

Those are the only words I retained.

I know now that the column of light, that pillar of brilliant energy, was Steve. Is Steve.

Unseen, but present.

In the now.

Already with thee.

[you're dead, aren't you?]

Two months after the accident. Early autumn.
Teaching Shakespeare. Prospero's lines echo. I
sit on my couch, a blanket wrapped around me.
Warmed by the fire. A candle lit. Photos of
Steve on the mantle. Noah sits on the facing
couch, reading.

Warmth, comfort, and blessings. Hints of joy.
And (also) profound sadness. A dialogue.
A dance, really.

Such stuff as dreams are made on.

And so to bed. With a sense of excitement.

I sleep knowing I am with Steve and wake filled
with something that I can't touch or explain, but
which comforts.

Life in a physical body is in time.

Life outside of the body is outside of time.

The communication that can occur after death is

a communication that is beyond or within words.

When I allow myself to be present to feel and

hear Steve, I feel true joy.

And exhaustion.

And it is sometimes sufficient.

Though not always.

10

presence in absence

[remembering : Whale watch]

It was 1985. Before we were us. Your brother
invited you to Provincetown, and you invited me.

You still refused to view me as anything other
than a friend.

I knew we would be together. I had a vision of
our home. I knew we'd have children.

I would fall asleep in your apartment and hope
you'd invite me to stay over. You didn't. How well
I recall you gently nudging my arm. Beth, you
said. You should head home. You'd help me out,
hail a cab, and send me home.

But now, Provincetown.

Your brother assumed we were in a relationship.

He gave us a room with one bed in his home by the bay. You didn't say we weren't together.

This was hopeful.

We went to the beach. I put on my bikini. I felt strong and desirable. I was 23 years old. You looked at me. In that way.

This was hopeful, too.

We went out for dinner and over dessert I told you about past boyfriends. Romances in England, in Amsterdam, in Paris. The lover I lived with in Long Beach. I watched something shift in you. A softening. A burgeoning tenderness. A curiosity.

This was hopeful, too.

And then we went on a whale watch. The ocean was rough and it was raining. No whales to be seen. We'd gone inside to escape the rain but both felt seasick so went out on deck for some air. And there, heads between our legs, curled up next to one another, around one another, tangled up in one another's arms, feeling violently ill, our romance began.

Back on shore, we walked to the house. And went upstairs. And then? A first hug. Then, a first kiss. Oh. The earth shook for me, because of this, because of us. My whole body electrified. Finally you were allowing yourself to love me.

[—us : together]

And eventually I began spending nights with you. Your bedroom had a queen-size bed, a down comforter. We'd cuddle in bed nights and watch Fred and Ginger in their own dancing romance. "Cheek to Cheek." "They Can't Take That Away from Me." Astaire danced up the walls and upside down.

You wooed me through Astaire.

Days, Billie Holiday played through the speakers in your living room, her voice seeping into my body.

I stretched out on your bed. This beauty? This love? It was a new thing for me. I'd had relationships, some healthier than others. But with you? Oh, with you I just was. I was me in my truth. Comfortable. Not the least bit self-conscious. You could look at me and I didn't feel anything but love. No judgment. No desire to be other than I was. I was just me. And that was good. Sprawled on the bed. Limbs outstretched. A great out breath. A profound and deep inner healing taking place. A sense of being okay. And of being at home.

One day there was a great storm—thunder, lightning. Sheets of rain. We rode the elevator down, and went outside. And I danced in the rain in Riverside Park while you watched. You wondered, how can this be? She's all I want. What is my hesitation?

Before we got together as lovers we were friends. We each had other partners. We were friends. We laughed. We walked a lot. And anytime I needed help (I passed out in Central

Park and in the hospital gave your name, I had
dirty laundry and needed a washing machine,
I needed a place to relax, good food to enjoy),
you were the one.

I remember our lunches. Big bowls of sprouts
and rice. You'd prepare our lunches and we'd
sit together on the couch and eat. We
used chopsticks.

Your feelings for me baffled you. You spoke
with your astrologer. You had him compare our
charts. You invited me to meet your therapist.
You took me with you to your energy healer.
You tried to match me up with your friend at
a new age retreat.

My desire for you overwhelmed me at times. I
longed for you. I was wild about you. You drove a
stick shift. You played piano and sang. You were

gentle and kind. And you made me laugh.

After we got together we played together as children, almost. When I'd head out to work I'd say, Hop in my pocket so we can be together all day. How I needed you and loved you. I wanted you with me always.

[—writing as a numinous act]

The word *nostalgia* originated in the late
eighteenth century: A longing for something
that once was a part of you but now is not. This
word appeared because of a need to name
something. The separation between the self
and the other, for example.

[—mind —forg'd manacles]

I dream I am trapped In a chrysalis. I try to break free, but can't. I am suffocating. Immobilized. The more I struggle the more I panic.

A chrysalis is a transitional, or preparatory step. A caterpillar makes its chrysalis and rests in the self-created darkness. At the right moment, it emerges as the butterfly.

William Blake

The chrysalis is self-created just like the *mind-forg'd manacles*, just like the (imagined) separation between the lover and longed for beloved other.

[ecstasy]

I dream of satyrs. Horned creatures, sublime, divine. Followers of Dionysus. Spirits of nature and power. The uncontrollable. The untamed. The unbounded, boundary-less. Neither god nor animal nor human. Wild.

Exultation.

Divine intoxication.

Ecstasy. Dionysian ex-stasis. Outside of equilibrium. Mad, even. As a means to the self. Look inside and know thyself. Dissolution of (false illusory?) boundaries. It is sublime. Sublimation derives from the Latin *sublimat* meaning to raise up. But it is also a term used in chemistry to describe the change of a solid substance directly into vapor, yet that reforms as a solid upon cooling.

This dance I live.

Sublime.

[*Flying, redux*]

Ari experiences connection and joy and transcendence in flight. Piloting the plane he renovated and flew with his father continues to help with the healing. He feels closer to his father in the plane.

For Noah the plane causes panic.

Steve saw Noah fly solo. But Noah didn't earn his license until after Steve's death. The plane causes Noah to feel isolated and completely alone, un-held, un-tethered. Like Ari, Noah is a skillful pilot, but alone in the plane he suffers profound grieving.

It reminds Noah of what he no longer has.

But he continues to fly and to try and recapture

the joy that flight represented for him. Despite the panic. In spite of the panic.

I dreamed.

Noah is flying. I am with Ari when his phone rings. It is Noah. He is lost.
He had accepted a dare from a flying buddy to fly blind—no map, no instruments. Nothing. He had to rely completely on his eyes. And he is lost.

Where is he, Ari?

That's the problem, Ari says. He doesn't know. And he doesn't know where to go.

Perhaps the most challenging aspect of readjustment is watching your children grieve and not being able to do anything to make it better. Save for loving them.

[imagining, again]

Resting in the void.

I want to wander through the pathless unmarked.

I walk hand in hand with another. We are dressed
in red, our steps slow and steady. We walk a
white, pure, pristine landscape, yet leave no
footprints. It is cold and snow-covered, level. At
the horizon, the blue of the sky meets the snow.

I see figures walking in the distance. As I move
closer I absorb the figures into myself and am
one with the landscape.
It is a painless process.

When Steve died a friend suggested I journal.
I wrote daily, usually more than once a day.
I wrote about my pain, my despair, my longing.

I wrote about our children. I wrote my fear. I wrote my dreams, and I wrote my visions, and the melodies I heard. I tried to silence my desire to force order from the chaos I lived and just be.

And take notes.

[*the ordinary*]

Memories of the daily. Unremarkable. Poignant.

Gabrielle's woolens. Ari's cloth diapers. Noah's woolens. Diaper deliveries. Rinse the diapers in the toilet, set the pail outside for the truck. New diapers arrive, fresh, white, unsullied.

In bed, Steve by my side, Gabrielle in my arms, nursing.

The skylight over our bed. Moonlight. Sunlight.

Set out the wooden trains in a basket. Gabrielle and Ari create a village marked by trains. Beeswax figures. Golden lions play with children.

The costume box. Dress up as princes and dancers. Knights, too.

Ari is born and Gabrielle runs in, holding her baby doll. She sits in the bed beside me, nursing her baby as I nurse Ari.

Ari sits on the broom while Steve sweeps the crumbs into the corner.

Snow overnight. Steve wakes early, puts on his boots, and heads out to shovel the steps and the driveway, to dig us out.

Steve sprouts alfalfa, clover, and radish. He makes a salad and tosses it with a tahini dressing. We have a wooden bowl Steve purchased in Mexico over twenty years before. We light the beeswax candles. All three children sit around the table that Steve had all those years ago in his Riverside Drive apartment. We hold hands, sing our grace, and eat. Night after night.

A night downtown. Dinner just the two of us.
Driving in the car, backing out of the driveway,
Ari and Gabrielle popping their heads up out of
the back seats. Laughing.

The surprise of Noah.

Driving, Gabrielle singing to Noah. Ari holding
his stash of keys.

Bathing them. Laundering their clothes. The
never-ending laundry. The shopping lists.
All the lists.

The fragments.

[signs]

In the early months after Steve's death, I saw
things that existed whether my eyes were open
or closed.

I saw a vibrant column of light. I saw it when
my eyes were open. I saw it when my eyes
were closed.

Steve showed me a web of hexagonal forms,
breathing somehow. Moving. Morphing.
Gossamer wings. Fragile. Ephemeral. Seemingly
flimsy, seemingly easily broken, seemingly easily
destroyed. But not flimsy at all. And not
easily seen.

It depends on the light.

11

rebirth

James Joyce,
*A Portrait of
the Artist as a
Young Man*

Welcome, O life! I go to encounter for the millionth time the reality of experience and to forge in the smithy of my soul the uncreated conscience of my race.

[quest]

The summer after Steve's death, the summer that
would have marked our thirtieth anniversary, I
decide to complete my Master of Arts degree
with a summer at Oxford University.

My children support this and we plan to meet in
Oxford for my graduation.

 It is a difficult departure. Ari and Noah walked
me into Kennedy Airport and when I said
goodbye at security I sobbed. I sat in the
unmoving plane for three hours until they finally
canceled the flight because of engine trouble.
Seven hours until the next flight.

At Heathrow, finally, I need coffee. I see kiosks
but don't stop. I find the bus terminal, note
the time for the next bus to Oxford. I drag my

luggage to the coffee shop, and order the coffee. I pay with the pounds that I'd found in Steve's wallet. Bags. Coffee. Jet-lag. I am anxious, disoriented, and feel exposed.

The bus is outside.

I board. And settle in. Coffee. A book.
The book remains unread.
I gaze out the window of the bus, but nothing registers. I'm here. I'm somewhere. I'm nowhere.

[*courage*]

I see glorious green fields, and yet it as if I am
not present in that bus. Thinking that pierces
emotion. An inability to be present and grateful.
An observer in my own life.

One definition of courage is strength in the face
of grief or loss. And it derives from the latin, *cor*,
meaning heart.

The journey to become the hero of my life
begins in despair and in a void.

[dream fragment]

Before I travel to Oxford, I dream.

I walk down an empty alleyway, stone buildings,
narrow street. Seems to be Oxford.

No people.
Sun.

Alone.

[*pearls*]

I feel raw, stripped bare.

I think of the oyster, crafting the (eventually)
luminous pearl.

From an irritant.

Grief as an irritant?

I think of myself as a child—vulnerable, open,
something attacked. I created a protective shield.

Steve saw me. I didn't. But Steve saw me.

The pearl. What is revealed is what was there
all along.

We become who we always were.

[alone]

Acute homesickness. Homesick at home.

Homesick away from home.

The ache continues in England.

But this is balanced by burgeoning excitement.
I am studying in Oxford, after all.

Wild movement between wretched longing for
what is not possible. And bliss.

My already poor sense of direction is even
worse in England. I have an underlying anxiety
about wandering and am unable to negotiate
decisions. I rely on friends and acquaintances.
I really have no clear sense of where I
am—in any respect.

The colleges that comprise Oxford University are walled. I board in Lincoln College, near the Bodleian, and down the road from Blackwell's Bookstore. It takes me two weeks to walk alone through the stone entryway and down the street to Blackwell's.

During the first week, I stay after class to have a conversation with the professor. My friends head out. We agree to meet at the Porter's Lodge. The class is held in an old building at Lady Margaret Hall. We meet in the professor's office, sit on soft chairs, eat biscuits, and drink coffee. We discuss Melville, Coleridge, and Whitman.

My grief is present. I am never certain what will reveal the despair. My vulnerability allows for an absorption of poetry and literature in a way I had never experienced. I need to let my professor know what I am struggling with. I feel like

Coleridge's Mariner, forced to tell and retell my tale of woe, or suffer an agony that could only be relieved by telling his story.

> *He holds him with his glittering eye—*
> *The Wedding-Guest stood still,*
> *And listens like a three years' child:*
> *The Mariner hath his will.*

> *The Wedding-Guest sat on a stone:*
> *He cannot choose but hear;*
> *And thus spake on that ancient man,*
> *The bright-eyed Mariner.*

My professor listens to my tale. In stillness.

Tale told, I head out. Turn right. Then, left. But which stairs? Within moments I am lost. The building is a labyrinth. Every turn is the wrong turn. Locked doors. Blank walls. There seems to be no one I can ask for help. I have no cell phone. I have no map. There is no one in that building.

I collapse in a stairwell. And I sob.

Eventually I stand up and keep moving.

Eventually I see people in an office.

A man and a woman.

I am lost, I say.

The man pulls out a map, marks where we were, and where I am looking to go. He says I'm not the only one to get lost.

It's a confusing building, he says, smiling.

Map in hand, I find my way to the Porter's Lodge.

But my friends have come and gone.

I walk through the park.

Looking for the jasmine flowers I had noticed

on my way in.

Trying to recall whether I have seen that

bench before.

Exiting onto the street. And looking for

Lincoln College.

I do find my way home. Back to the college.

Physically. Emotionally. Spent.

[—melville musing]

The first book we read this Oxford summer
is *Moby-Dick*.

Call me Ishmael.
Call me the one who hears.
Call me the one who has heard God.
Call me the one who has been heard by God.

I am Ishmael. I set myself the challenge of
connection, or of reintegration. But I am also
Ahab, trapped in my own perception.

Life is a voyage. And to understand any one
thing, you need to understand it all.

By attentiveness to detail, the correspondence to
the whole emerges.

There is always a thread to hold onto, connecting to all.

Losing the self in the immensities. What can I hold onto? Climb the rigging. The wind blows. I try to hold and let go. Both.

I am the sailor perched high above in the crow's nest. Moving with the rhythm of the sea. Not falling. Not drowning.

Not lost in the immensities. Not lost in the prison of the self.

I look out over the sea. Where is home?

Living with the what ifs but not lost there, not remaining there.

Ahab's self-created narcissistic perception of the

world is perplexing, somehow retarding.

I reject Ahab.

But I understand him.

Poor me? Perhaps not so poor after all. True,
I experienced the awful lonesomeness of the
self without boundaries. But I also see the
foundational elements that comprise existence.
I see the elements of chaos.

The realm of potential.

So? I go to sea.

Is the sea the uncharted/unchartable? What is
it about entering the boundless that can allow
for a glimpse into the essence of things, for an
experiencing of the nothingness that is, in
truth, something?

Ishmael goes to sea. He looks to lose himself. But also Ishmael attempts to classify chaos so as to find some way of orienting himself. Launching into his story, he attempts to include everything about the sea and the whale and whaling. I try to orient myself and find myself writing about Keats and my childhood, and birds.

[—presence]

How I know Steve is near:

1. A gentle pressure, or sometimes a slight tingling, inside my head. On the right side.
2. I feel an energy surge. Sometimes I even have to move, dancing around.
3. I hear a song in my head. And then when I play the song my whole body agrees. Sometimes I dance then, too.
4. I hear a song and I close my eyes. "Love is Here to Stay." "They Can't Take That Away From Me." "Come Rain or Come Shine." I feel Steve.
5. A palpable visceral sense of joy comes over me. Total ecstasy. (The same joy I felt at the funeral.)
6. I see a red-tailed hawk.
7. I see a crow.

8. I see butterflies. Usually monarch.

9. I feel compelled to look up at the sky. *Look up, Bud*. That's what I hear. Look up and out.

10. I feel a wave of despair, and right then a friend calls.

11. I see colors that move and morph and dance. Whether my eyes are opened or closed. Golden/green. Sometimes rose red.

12. I discover a sudden unexpected like for fresh green juices. When I drink, I feel a burst of Steve.

13. I sprout peas and alfalfa, radish, broccoli. For the first time. And I hear, *Yay, Bud*.

14. I feel beautiful.

15. During savasana, I experience what I imagine Steve felt when he left his body—a floating sensation, a weightlessness, a freedom.

I listen. And I notice. And I breathe into the pause offered.

[The chair]

It becomes a pilgrimage. The summer in Oxford.
The visit to Keats's home in London.

Hampstead Heath is a day trip from Oxford.

Emily and I take the bus into London and the
Tube to Hampstead. We walk the tree-lined
streets, past the lush green heath.

At Keats's house, I sit on the front steps for a
photo. I knock my glasses off, don't realize, and
when I stand up, step on the glasses, shattering
them, my disorientation made manifest.

I sit on Keats's chair, the one in Joseph Severn's
painting. Keats sits perched lightly on the edge
of the chair, his head resting on his left hand.
His arm is on another chair. His legs are crossed.

A sheaf of papers on his lap. I believe he's supposed to be writing "Ode to a Nightingale."

Emily takes a series of photos of me trying to sit as Keats did. I feel enormous in that tiny chair. I think it will break.

The stairs are narrow. My feet feel huge, too big to maneuver. And no glasses now. Walking up the stairs to his bedroom, to his beloved Fanny's bedroom, I stumble.

The entire house is small. Low ceilings. Narrow hallways.

I see the bed that Keats slept in. I stand beside the pillow. The ceiling is low. I bow my head.

On the grass in the yard, under the trees.

I close my eyes. No nightingale, but peace.

I hold a death mask of the young poet.

[*graduation*]

The summer in Oxford is a turning point.

As co-president of my graduating class I am
asked to speak at graduation. All I can think
about is honoring Steve and our children, and
expressing my gratitude to my classmates
and instructors.

I stand in the chapel. Built in 1629. Two rows of
hard wooden benches mark a narrow central
aisle. There sit Gabrielle, Ari, and Noah. And
my friends. To get to the pew, I need to walk
down the aisle. Stained glass windows depicting
scenes from the life of Jesus and from the Old
Testament allow for a hushed light.

I begin.

Try to somehow honor every individual present.

Samuel Beckett I speak about a class where we read "Worstword Ho." The instructor felt he couldn't understand Beckett's work without approaching it as a community.

So we read it as a community. Every student read a paragraph.

Initially uncomfortable, with a bit of trepidation and awkward pauses, we found our way in. We listened to the words of Beckett and to the voices of our classmates. The text came alive. We created a vessel that Beckett's words could live within and emanate from.

When we finished reading Beckett, the room was filled with a silence that seemed vitalized

somehow. It felt as if we had performed
a sacrament.

Behind the podium, I speak about Steve's car
accident and how in the confusion of those early
days what kept arising out of a mist, almost,
were words from Keats—*Though the dull brain
perplexes and retards/Already with thee!*

I explain that Keats had always been a favorite of
mine, but I now recognized that his poetry and
the notion of liminality are more than intellectual
constructs. The poetry became the way I moved
from incomprehension and confusion to some
sense of peace and acceptance.

And then I close with Beckett.

> *On. Say on. Be said on. Somehow on.*
> *Till nohow on. Said nohow on.*

Say for be said. Missaid. From now say
for missaid.

Say a body. Where none. No mind.
Where none. That at least. A place.
Where none. For the body. To be in.
Move in. Out of. Back into. No. No out.
No back. Only in. Stay in. On in. Still.

All of old. Nothing else ever. Ever tried.
Ever failed. No matter. Try again. Fail
again. Fail better.

[*Tutelage*]

I am on a quest. I need to find the object lost. This necessitates a journey within. I seek the home I have lost. I need to carry a sack. I need good sturdy walking shoes. I need a walking stick carved from a willow tree.

I need to be prepared. Here's what I need:

- A friend, or two
- A writing tool and paper, or computer
- Coffee
- Steve
- Memories
- The liminal
- Trust
- Steve
- Breadcrumbs
- A cloak

- Humility
- Listening
- The child
- The crone
- Strong heart
- Fire
- Warrior courage
- Strength
- Balance

I need no map. There is no map.

The journey is unmarked but decipherable. I can find my way home. All I need to do is recall and remember. Re/member the self, and the puzzle and confusion and isolation ends.

Tutelage defined as keeping and as being watched over.

Tutelage assumes protection and guidance. It is a liminal construct. Because although protection can be—and usually is—something tangible, it often isn't. It is both. And the tutelage offered on this subliminal level is profound and true.

And eternal.

[crashes redux]

You step on the glass at our wedding and
it shatters.

I throw a glass against stones and it shatters,
some of the shards so small that I can't see them.

The end of something, but the beginning of
something, too.

A plane crash. A car crash.
Both.

You biked over the George Washington Bridge
from your home in the Bronx to Teterboro
Airport. You were seventeen years old.

Your parents were not unsupportive, you said,
but they wanted no part in this passion of yours.

If you were to fly, you would need to pay for it, and arrange lessons.

To earn money you played piano in bars. Underage. Not allowed to drink, but permitted to entertain.

Whenever you had the money, you biked to the airport. To learn to fly.

A big draw in moving to the Berkshires were two small airports.

Gabrielle and Ari were both under the age of five. I was studying in New Hampshire. You were taking them for a flight to visit their grandparents. You were a passenger for the first leg. Focused on your children, not on the pilot. Who made an error.

A midair collision.

Your plane's wheels locked onto the other

plane's wing.

Tumbling together one thousand feet.

Flipping over on the ground.

The fuselage crumpled.

Broken windows.

Pulling yourself and our children to safety.

Ari and Gabrielle spoke of angels lowering

the plane.

Neither child experienced fear.

But you did.

And I did.

The space between these two crashes is a life—

twenty-one years. Time for those two young

children to go to elementary school, then high

school, and then college and travel. Time for a third child to be born. Time to move to a larger house, renovate, and rebuild. Time to experience a marriage in all its vicissitudes. Bonus years. After the first crash.

And until the second crash.

12

re/membered

[*interlude : The Boxer*]

I find boxing.

Jab jab, cross.

Upper cut.

Step.

Step.

Step, jab.

Step back, jab.

Focus. Focus, Beth.

Moving through. Reacting. Catch what comes.

Return to center. Knowing I can handle

what comes.

I dance.

I discover my power. My speed.

I am light. Yet firmly planted. Knowing the ground holds me.

I move through anything that retards. I break through false boundaries. Illusory walls.

[—the fool]

I am the fool. I am the hero of this journey,
whether I want to be or not.
I stand at the edge of a cliff, smiling, gazing
at landscape varied and dynamic—mountains,
valleys, rivers. I am above the clouds. One step
and I am off the edge, but I am not worried. I
have all I need in a small bundle tied with twine
and bound to a stick. My companion, a small
pup, stands at my left side. Any fear about my
next move passes through me.

I am prepared to step into the unknown.
Another beginning.

[present movement]

I am in the living room, sitting on the couch. The
three children are here, cooking and laughing in
the kitchen. I hear the sounds of pots and pans,
dishes, slamming cabinets. I smell garlic
and spices.

I'm coming, I say.

[acknowledgements]

You helped me negotiate this unsought for path.
I could not have made it through without you.

Gabrielle. Ari. Noah.

Jordyn. Danielle. Liz. Cathy. Genève. Alison.
Winslow. Ed.

So many more.

Devon and Meryl for your generosity in giving
this book form.

My mother and father, my sister and brother, and
brothers-in-law and sisters-in-law.

Emily Bartels and Bread Loaf School of English at
Middlebury College, for friendship, intellectual

and creative stimulation, and encouragement.

Christine Gerrard for allowing me to begin
to break form that summer in Oxford and put
myself in conversation with my poets.

Rabbis Jodi Gordon and Neil Hirsch, Janet Lee,
and Hevreh of Southern Berkshire for catching
and carrying us through those early weeks,
and beyond.

Steve Sagarin and the Berkshire Waldorf High
School community for your presence and
generosity throughout all of this.

And to Steve. For saying yes.

[addendum]

The poems and the poets provide the
scaffolding. And help me feel less isolated.

The alienation that seems an inescapable
part of life as a physical being is addressed
and transformed through development of the
capacities Keats espouses—and even if one
cannot live as fully present to the other as Keats,
it seems a worthwhile response to the sense
of loss and of disconnection. To write about a
nightingale in the form of the ode, Keats makes
a radical statement. The ode was a lyric poem of
praise to a person, thing, or event not present.
Keats praises a particular nightingale who is very
much present, yet by moving into the truth of
that particular bird, he touches on something
not at all present physically, and yet very real.
It is in a moment of darkness or disorientation,

or confrontation with a void or an abyss, that the possibility emerges for a reconnection with the desired goal, whether a nightingale, or a memory. The universal is discovered through a true seeing of the particular.

Ode to a Nightingale

by John Keats

My heart aches, and a drowsy numbness pains

    My sense, as though of hemlock I had drunk,

Or emptied some dull opiate to the drains

    One minute past, and Lethe-wards had sunk:

'Tis not through envy of thy happy lot,

    But being too happy in thine happiness,—

        That thou, light-winged Dryad of the trees

           In some melodious plot

    Of beechen green, and shadows numberless,

        Singest of summer in full-throated ease.

O, for a draught of vintage! that hath been

    Cool'd a long age in the deep-delved earth,

Tasting of Flora and the country green,

    Dance, and Provençal song, and sunburnt mirth!

O for a beaker full of the warm South,

    Full of the true, the blushful Hippocrene,

With beaded bubbles winking at the brim,

    And purple-stained mouth;

That I might drink, and leave the world unseen,

    And with thee fade away into the forest dim:

Fade far away, dissolve, and quite forget

    What thou among the leaves hast never known,

The weariness, the fever, and the fret

    Here, where men sit and hear each other groan;

Where palsy shakes a few, sad, last gray hairs,

    Where youth grows pale, and spectre-thin, and dies;

    Where but to think is to be full of sorrow

        And leaden-eyed despairs,

    Where Beauty cannot keep her lustrous eyes,

    Or new Love pine at them beyond to-morrow.

Away! away! for I will fly to thee,

    Not charioted by Bacchus and his pards,

But on the viewless wings of Poesy,

    Though the dull brain perplexes and retards:

Already with thee! tender is the night,

    And haply the Queen-Moon is on her throne,

        Cluster'd around by all her starry Fays;

            But here there is no light,

    Save what from heaven is with the breezes blown

        Through verdurous glooms and winding mossy ways.

I cannot see what flowers are at my feet,

    Nor what soft incense hangs upon the boughs,

But, in embalmed darkness, guess each sweet

    Wherewith the seasonable month endows

The grass, the thicket, and the fruit-tree wild;

    White hawthorn, and the pastoral eglantine;

        Fast fading violets cover'd up in leaves;

            And mid-May's eldest child,

    The coming musk-rose, full of dewy wine,

        The murmurous haunt of flies on summer eves.

Darkling I listen; and, for many a time

    I have been half in love with easeful Death,

Call'd him soft names in many a mused rhyme,

To take into the air my quiet breath;

Now more than ever seems it rich to die,

To cease upon the midnight with no pain,

While thou art pouring forth thy soul abroad

In such an ecstasy!

Still wouldst thou sing, and I have ears in vain—

To thy high requiem become a sod.

Thou wast not born for death, immortal Bird!

No hungry generations tread thee down;

The voice I hear this passing night was heard

In ancient days by emperor and clown:

Perhaps the self-same song that found a path

Through the sad heart of Ruth, when, sick for home,

She stood in tears amid the alien corn;

The same that oft-times hath

Charm'd magic casements, opening on the foam

Of perilous seas, in faery lands forlorn.

Forlorn! the very word is like a bell

    To toll me back from thee to my sole self!

Adieu! the fancy cannot cheat so well

    As she is fam'd to do, deceiving elf.

Adieu! adieu! thy plaintive anthem fades

    Past the near meadows, over the still stream,

        Up the hill-side; and now 'tis buried deep

           In the next valley-glades:

    Was it a vision, or a waking dream?

        Fled is that music:—Do I wake or sleep?

Selections from Walt Whitman, "Song of Myself"

I depart as air . . . I shake my white locks at the runaway sun,
I effuse my flesh in eddies and drift it in lacy jags.

I bequeath myself to the dirt to grow from the grass I love,
If you want me again look for me under your bootsoles.

You will hardly know who I am or what I mean,
But I shall be good health to you nevertheless,
And filter and fibre your blood.

Failing to fetch me at first keep encouraged,
Missing me one place search another,
I stop somewhere waiting for you

more Whitman:

They are alive and well somewhere;
The smallest sprout shows there is really no death,

And if ever there was it led forward life,

   and does not wait at the end to arrest it,

And ceased the moment life appeared.

All goes onward and outward . . . and nothing collapses,

And to die is different from what any one supposed, and luckier

[selected works cited]

Coleridge, S. T. *Coleridge's Poetry and Prose*.
New York: W. W. Norton & Company. 2004.

Dante Alighieri, Robert Pinsky. *The Inferno of
Dante*. New York: Farrar, Straus and
Giroux. 1994.

Dickinson, Emily. *The Complete Poems of
Emily Dickinson*. Boston, MA: Little, Brown and
Company. 1961.

Dillard, Annie. *Pilgrim at Tinker Creek*. New York:
Harper Perennial Modern Classics. 2013.

Emerson, Ralph Waldo. *The Essential Writings of
Ralph Waldo Emerson*. New York: The Modern
Library. 2000.

Keats, John. *Keats's Poetry and Prose*. New York:

    W. W. Norton & Company. 2009.

Whitman, Walt. *Leaves of Grass*. The Original

    1855 Edition. Mineola, NY: Dover Thrift

    Editions. 2007.

Wordsworth, William. *The Prelude*. New York: W.

    W. Norton & Company. 1979.

Beth Robbins is a longtime English and drama teacher at the Berkshire Waldorf High School in Stockbridge, MA. Prior to that, she worked as an editor for SteinerBooks/ Anthroposophic Press. She found her voice as a writer while studying at Oxford University through the Bread Loaf School of English program which she attended after the sudden death of her husband. In 2017, the Bread Loaf Journal published her personal essay–"Fragments in Liminality: A Lover's Discourse," which has since been expanded into her first book, *A Grief Sublime* (Keats & Company Publishers, 2019). She teaches and lives in the Berkshires of Western Massachusetts, and continues to discourse with Dickinson, Whitman, Emerson, and, of course, Keats.

bethrobbins.co